The Property Risk Handbook (Standard Edition)

The Complete Homebuyer's Guide to Understanding Hidden Home Hazards Beyond the Inspection

Damian Martinez

AMADO MEDIA GROUP

Amado Media Group

Standard Edition – First Edition - December 2025

Published by Damian Martinez

For important legal disclaimers and limitations of liability, see the Legal Disclaimer section of this book.

HomeDataReports.com

Printed in the United States of America

Book Dedication

For those who believe the American Dream should be built on truth, not surprises: may you discover what lies beneath the listing photos and buy with complete clarity, confidence, and conviction.

Scan for your FREE property risk report
homedatareports.com/books

Legal Disclaimer

Please Read Carefully Before Using This Book

No Professional Relationship or Advisory Services

The information contained in this book is provided strictly for educational and informational purposes. By reading this book, you acknowledge and agree that:

The author is NOT:

A licensed real estate agent, broker, or real estate professional

A licensed attorney or legal professional providing legal advice

A licensed insurance agent or broker providing insurance advice

A certified financial advisor, planner, or investment professional

A licensed home inspector or property inspector

A licensed engineer, geologist, environmental consultant, or contractor

A licensed appraiser or real estate evaluator

An employee, contractor, or affiliate of any federal, state, or local government agency

Nothing in this book creates any professional advisory relationship between you and the author, including but not limited to attorney-client, agent-client, advisor-client, or any other fiduciary relationship.

Educational Purpose and Scope

This book is designed to educate prospective homebuyers about property risk analysis methodologies using publicly available federal databases and government resources. The content teaches readers:

How to access publicly available federal data from agencies including FEMA, NOAA, USGS, EPA, and the U.S. Census Bureau

How to interpret flood zone designations, seismic hazard maps, environmental proximity data, and climate projections

How to evaluate location-based risks not typically covered in standard home inspections

How to incorporate risk data into property evaluation and negotiation strategies

This book is NOT intended to:

Provide specific advice about any particular property or transaction

Replace professional guidance from licensed real estate, legal, insurance, financial, or inspection professionals

Discourage or prevent home purchases in any specific location, risk zone, or geographic area

Serve as a substitute for professional property inspections, appraisals, environmental assessments, or engineering evaluations

Guarantee specific outcomes, financial results, or risk predictions

Offer insurance underwriting opinions or coverage recommendations

Provide legal opinions about disclosure requirements, contract terms, or liability issues

Understanding Property Risk — All Properties Carry Risk

Critical Acknowledgment:

The author explicitly acknowledges that **every residential property carries some level of risk**—whether from natural hazards (flood, wildfire, earthquake, hurricane), environmental factors (contamination, radon, air quality), market conditions (property values, insurance availability), demographic trends, or structural/mechanical conditions.

The Purpose of This Book:

This book is NOT designed to steer readers away from properties with documented risks. Rather, the purpose is to help readers:

Understand the specific risks associated with a property using publicly available federal data

Evaluate whether those risks align with their personal circumstances, risk tolerance, financial capacity, and long-term goals

Make informed decisions about risk acceptance, mitigation strategies, insurance planning, and financial preparation

Negotiate intelligently using documented data rather than assumptions or incomplete information

Risk Acceptance is a Personal Decision:

A property located in a FEMA-designated flood zone, wildfire hazard area, seismic zone, hurricane region, or near environmental concerns may still be an excellent choice for many buyers—**if they understand the risks, plan accordingly, budget for associated costs, and make fully informed decisions.**

The decision to accept, mitigate, or reject specific risks is entirely personal and depends on:

Individual financial capacity and budget flexibility

Personal risk tolerance and comfort level with uncertainty

Long-term ownership plans and investment horizon

Insurance availability and affordability in the specific location

Ability and willingness to invest in mitigation measures

Family circumstances, health considerations, and lifestyle preferences

Mandatory Professional Consultation

YOU MUST consult with appropriate licensed professionals before making any real estate purchase, financial commitment, insurance decision, or legal agreement.

Required Professional Consultations Include:

Real Estate Professionals:

Licensed real estate attorney for contract review, disclosure analysis, title examination, and legal protections specific to your transaction and jurisdiction

Licensed real estate agent or broker for market analysis, property valuation, negotiation strategy, and transaction guidance

Property Assessment Professionals:

Licensed home inspector for comprehensive evaluation of property condition, systems, and structural integrity

Licensed contractors, engineers, or specialists for foundation assessment, structural evaluation, environmental testing, or geological analysis as needed

Licensed appraiser for independent market value assessment (typically required by mortgage lenders)

Insurance Professionals:

Licensed insurance agent or broker for accurate insurance quotes, coverage options, policy requirements, carrier availability, and risk assessment

Multiple insurance quotes from different carriers to understand market conditions and pricing variability

Financial Professionals:

Certified financial advisor for affordability analysis, mortgage guidance, long-term financial planning, and investment strategy

Qualified tax professional for property tax implications, deductibility questions, and financial consequences

Mortgage lender or loan officer for financing options, qualification requirements, and loan terms

Specialized Consultants (as needed):

Environmental consultants for Phase I/II Environmental Site Assessments near industrial areas, Superfund sites, or contamination concerns

Geotechnical engineers for soil analysis, foundation evaluation, or seismic retrofit recommendations

Flood mitigation specialists for elevation certificates, LOMA applications, or flood protection strategies

Wildfire mitigation consultants for defensible space planning or fire-resistant construction in high-risk areas

The author strongly recommends retaining qualified professionals licensed in your specific jurisdiction before making any property-related decisions.

Data Sources, Currency, and Limitations

Federal Data Sources

The information in this book is based on publicly available federal databases and government resources, including but not limited to:

FEMA (Federal Emergency Management Agency): Flood Insurance Rate Maps (FIRMs), Special Flood Hazard Areas (SFHAs), Base Flood Elevations (BFE), disaster declarations, National Flood Insurance Program (NFIP) data

NOAA (National Oceanic and Atmospheric Administration): Climate data, sea-level rise projections, storm surge models, hurricane historical data, precipitation trends

USGS (United States Geological Survey): Seismic hazard maps, earthquake probability models, fault line locations, geological surveys, sinkhole data, landslide inventories

EPA (Environmental Protection Agency): Superfund (NPL) site locations, Toxic Release Inventory (TRI), RCRA hazardous waste facilities, underground storage tanks (USTs), air and water quality data, radon zone maps

U.S. Census Bureau: Demographic data, economic indicators, population trends, housing statistics, neighborhood characteristics

Data Currency and Update Frequency

CRITICAL LIMITATION:

Federal databases are updated on varying schedules. FEMA flood maps may be revised every 5-10 years in some areas or remain unchanged for decades in others. USGS seismic hazard maps are updated approximately every 6 years. EPA Superfund listings change as sites are added, remediated, or delisted. NOAA climate projections are revised as modeling improves.

The author makes NO GUARANTEE that any data, statistic, map designation, risk assessment, example, or recommendation in this book:

Remains current or accurate at the time you read it

Applies to the specific property you are considering

Reflects the most recent federal database updates

Matches information provided by local jurisdictions

Aligns with private-sector risk modeling or insurance underwriting

YOUR RESPONSIBILITY:

You are solely responsible for independently verifying ALL information with:

Current federal databases (FEMA, NOAA, USGS, EPA, Census)

State and local government agencies with jurisdiction over the property

Licensed professionals familiar with current market conditions

Insurance carriers regarding actual coverage availability and pricing

Mortgage lenders regarding current underwriting standards

Forward-Looking Projections and Probabilistic Risk Assessment

Nature of Risk Modeling

This book discusses forward-looking risk projections, including but not limited to:

Climate change impacts over 10, 20, and 30-year periods
Sea-level rise scenarios and coastal flooding projections
Wildfire risk expansion based on vegetation, climate, and development patterns
Earthquake probability models and ground shaking estimates
Hurricane intensity and frequency projections
Long-term property value trends and market dynamics

CRITICAL DISCLAIMER:

All forward-looking risk assessments are **probabilistic models based on historical data, scientific assumptions, and computational projections.** They are NOT guarantees, predictions, or certainties about future events.

Limitations of Risk Modeling:

Models Change: Scientific understanding evolves. Today's "best available science" may be revised or replaced as new data emerges.

Probability is Not Destiny: A property with a "1% annual flood risk" (100-year floodplain) may flood multiple times in a decade—or never flood in a century. Probability describes likelihood, not inevitability.

Unexpected Events Occur: Hurricane Helene (2024) caused catastrophic flooding in North Carolina mountain areas previously considered "no flood risk." Models cannot predict every scenario.

Local Conditions Matter: Federal models provide general risk assessments. Specific property characteristics (elevation, drainage, construction, mitigation) can significantly alter actual risk.

Climate Uncertainty: Long-term climate projections depend on greenhouse gas emission scenarios, policy decisions, technological changes, and feedback loops that remain uncertain.

Accuracy Disputes:

The real estate industry, insurance carriers, and property owners have disputed the accuracy of climate risk models and forward-looking projections. In December 2024, Zillow removed detailed climate risk data from property listings after pressure from real estate agents and the California Regional MLS (CRMLS), who argued that risk scores were:

"Arbitrary and inaccurate"
"Stigmatizing properties based on uncertain projections"
"Causing deals to fall apart unfairly"

The author acknowledges that:

Risk modeling involves judgment, assumptions, and uncertainty
Different models may produce different risk assessments for the same property
Industry stakeholders have financial incentives to minimize or contest risk data
Buyers must make their own informed judgments about acceptable risk levels

YOU ASSUME ALL RISK associated with relying on forward-looking projections, risk models, or probabilistic assessments discussed in this book.

Insurance Considerations and the Current Market Crisis

The Insurance Availability Crisis (2024-2025)

As documented in this book and widely reported in financial media, the United States residential property insurance market is experiencing a structural crisis characterized by:

Major carriers (State Farm, Allstate, Farmers) retreating from high-risk states including California, Florida, and Louisiana

Premium increases of 20-50%+ annually in hurricane, wildfire, and flood-prone areas

Increasing reliance on state-run "insurers of last resort" (FAIR Plans, Citizens Property Insurance)

Tightened underwriting standards excluding properties previously eligible for coverage

Reduced coverage limits and increased deductibles in high-risk zones

Critical Insurance Disclaimers

The author is NOT a licensed insurance agent or broker and provides NO insurance advice.

This book discusses insurance considerations as part of property risk analysis, including:

How to obtain insurance quotes before making purchase offers

How flood zones, wildfire risk, and seismic hazards affect insurance availability

How to evaluate insurance costs as part of long-term ownership expenses

How to identify properties that may be difficult or impossible to insure

HOWEVER:

The author CANNOT and DOES NOT predict whether any specific property will be insurable

Insurance carrier decisions are proprietary and change frequently based on internal risk models

A property "insurable today" may become uninsurable tomorrow if carriers exit the market

Actual insurance premiums depend on factors beyond the scope of this book (credit scores, claims history, coverage limits, deductibles, bundling, discounts)

Insurance coverage gaps, exclusions, and limitations vary by policy and carrier

YOUR RESPONSIBILITY:

You MUST obtain actual insurance quotes from licensed agents or brokers for ANY property you are seriously considering. Do NOT rely on:

Generic premium estimates or averages provided in this book

Insurance costs paid by previous owners (rates change)

Assumptions about coverage availability based on risk data alone

If you cannot secure affordable insurance coverage for a property, you should NOT proceed with the purchase unless you are financially prepared to self-insure against total loss.

Mortgage lenders WILL require proof of insurance before closing. A property that cannot be insured typically cannot be mortgaged.

State, Local, and Regional Variation

Legal and Regulatory Differences

Real estate laws, disclosure requirements, insurance regulations, building codes, environmental standards, and market practices **vary significantly by state, county, municipality, and even within local jurisdictions.**

Examples of Variation:

Disclosure Laws: California requires Natural Hazard Disclosure Statements. Florida requires sinkhole and flood zone disclosure. Texas has minimal mandatory disclosure. Many states follow "as-is" or "buyer beware" traditions with limited seller obligations.

Flood Insurance Requirements: Mandatory for mortgaged properties in FEMA Special Flood Hazard Areas (SFHAs) nationwide, but some local jurisdictions require disclosure of flood history, previous claims, or elevation certificates.

Wildfire Building Codes: California has strict defensible space requirements and fire-resistant construction standards in Fire Hazard Severity Zones. Other states may have minimal or no wildfire-specific regulations.

Environmental Disclosure: Some states require disclosure of known contamination, underground storage tanks, or proximity to Superfund sites. Others do not.

Seismic Standards: California has strict earthquake retrofit requirements for certain building types. Other seismically active states (Washington, Utah, Missouri) have varying standards.

YOU MUST:

Research the specific laws, regulations, and disclosure requirements in your state, county, and municipality

Consult with local licensed professionals (attorneys, agents, inspectors) familiar with your jurisdiction

Verify that any guidance, strategy, or example in this book complies with local legal requirements

Understand that examples from one location may not apply to your specific situation

The author provides general educational information and CANNOT account for thousands of variations in laws, regulations, and practices across the United States.

No Guarantee of Results or Outcomes

What This Book Does NOT Guarantee

Following the guidance, strategies, or methodologies in this book does NOT guarantee:

That you will find a suitable property or avoid all risks

That you will negotiate a lower purchase price or favorable contract terms

That you will save money on insurance, taxes, or long-term ownership costs

That property values will appreciate or remain stable

That you will successfully appeal a FEMA flood map designation or risk classification

That mitigation measures will be effective or reduce insurance premiums

That you will avoid property damage from natural disasters or environmental hazards

That climate risk projections will accurately predict future conditions

Any specific financial, legal, insurance, or real estate outcome

Real estate transactions involve numerous variables beyond the scope of this book, including:

Market conditions (supply, demand, interest rates, economic trends)

Individual property characteristics (age, condition, location, features)

Seller motivations, competing offers, and negotiation dynamics

Lender underwriting standards and mortgage approval requirements

Inspection findings, appraisal results, and title issues

Insurance carrier availability and underwriting decisions

Regulatory changes, zoning amendments, and development projects

Natural disasters, economic downturns, and unforeseen events

YOUR RESULTS WILL VARY based on your specific circumstances, the property you choose, the professionals you hire, market conditions at the time of purchase, and countless other factors outside the author's control.

Limitation of Liability

Maximum Legal Protection

To the maximum extent permitted by law, the author, publisher, HomeDataRepor ts.com, PropertyRiskReports.com, and any affiliated companies, websites, or subsidiaries **disclaim all liability and responsibility** for any loss, damage, injury, financial harm, or adverse outcome arising from or related to:

Use of Information:

Use, misuse, reliance on, or inability to use information in this book

Decisions made based on this book's content, examples, strategies, or recommendations

Errors, omissions, inaccuracies, or outdated information in the book

Misinterpretation or misunderstanding of concepts, data, or methodologies

Data and Risk Assessment:

Changes in federal data, flood maps, climate projections, or risk assessments after publication

Reliance on forward-looking projections, risk models, or probabilistic assessments

Differences between information in this book and current federal database data

Inaccuracies or limitations in federal databases, government maps, or agency data

Variations between federal data and local jurisdiction information

Market and Industry Changes:

Changes in insurance markets, carrier availability, premium pricing, or coverage terms

Changes in real estate market conditions, property values, or buyer demand

Regulatory changes, disclosure law amendments, or new legal requirements

Industry resistance to transparency or risk data (as occurred with Zillow in December 2024)

Professional Services:

Failure to consult licensed professionals before making decisions

Advice, opinions, or services provided by third-party professionals you retain

Conflicts between this book's guidance and professional advice you receive

Actions or inactions of real estate agents, attorneys, inspectors, lenders, or insurance agents

Property-Specific Outcomes:

Property damage from floods, fires, earthquakes, hurricanes, or other natural disasters

Insurance coverage denials, premium increases, or carrier non-renewals

Inability to secure insurance coverage or mortgage financing

Property value declines, market downturns, or loss of equity

Unexpected repair costs, maintenance expenses, or mitigation investments

Disclosure issues, legal disputes, or transaction complications

YOU ASSUME ALL RISK associated with:

Using the information in this book to make property-related decisions

Relying on federal data, risk assessments, or forward-looking projections

Purchasing property in flood zones, wildfire areas, seismic zones, hurricane regions, or near environmental concerns

Accepting, mitigating, or attempting to manage property-related risks

Industry Context and Market Dynamics

Real Estate Industry Resistance to Risk Transparency

Critical Market Context:

The real estate industry has demonstrated resistance to comprehensive property risk transparency. As documented in financial and industry media:

December 2024 Zillow Climate Data Removal:

Zillow removed detailed climate risk scores from property listings after pressure from the California Regional MLS (CRMLS) and real estate agents who argued that:

Risk data was "killing deals" and reducing transaction volume

Climate scores were "arbitrary, inaccurate, and stigmatizing"

Properties in high-risk areas were being unfairly labeled

This removal occurred despite the data being sourced from First Street Foundation, a well-funded climate risk modeling company with $46+ million in venture capital and partnerships with NOAA, FEMA, and academic institutions.

Redfin's Contrarian Stance:

Redfin publicly committed to maintaining climate risk transparency on property listings, stating that buyers "deserve to know" about flood, fire, heat, wind, and air quality risks before making offers.

Industry Incentive Structure:

Real estate agents, brokers, and platforms earn commissions based on closed transactions. Risk transparency that reduces transaction volume or complicates deal closures creates financial disincentives for industry stakeholders.

What This Means for Readers

The author's approach in this book—comprehensive risk transparency using federal data—aligns with consumer interests but may conflict with industry preferences.

You should be aware that:

Real estate professionals may downplay or dismiss risk data discussed in this book

Industry stakeholders may have financial incentives to minimize risk concerns

Agents may pressure buyers to "not overthink" risk factors or "trust the process"

Forward-looking risk projections remain controversial and contested

However:

You have the right to access and use publicly available federal data

Risk transparency helps you make informed decisions aligned with YOUR interests, not industry transaction volume goals

Walking away from a high-risk property is a legitimate, responsible decision—not "being difficult"

Buyers who prioritize risk analysis may encounter resistance, but that does not invalidate the approach

The author believes buyers deserve complete transparency about property risks, even if that transparency complicates or prevents some transactions.

No Endorsement or Affiliation with Government Agencies

Independent Educational Content

This book references federal databases and government agencies including FEMA, NOAA, USGS, EPA, and the U.S. Census Bureau. **However:**

The author is NOT employed by, contracted with, or affiliated with any federal, state, or local government agency

This book is NOT endorsed, sponsored, or approved by FEMA, NOAA, USGS, EPA, Census Bureau, or any other government entity

Government agencies did NOT review, approve, or validate this book's content

The methodologies, interpretations, and recommendations in this book are the author's own and do NOT represent official government positions

Federal agencies provide raw data; they do NOT provide guidance on how to use that data for property purchasing decisions. The author's educational framework for interpreting and applying federal data is **independent and proprietary.**

Proprietary Methodology and Competitive Context

Novel Educational Approach

As documented in independent market research (December 2025), **no single consumer-facing product currently aggregates all major property risk categories—climate, environmental, crime, school safety, sex offender registry, and economic indicators—into comprehensive, affordable reports accessible to individual homebuyers.**

This book teaches a comprehensive risk analysis methodology that:

Integrates data from 10+ federal sources

Addresses gaps in standard home inspections

Provides frameworks for risk evaluation and negotiation

Offers strategies for long-term property intelligence monitoring

This approach is unique in the consumer real estate education market.

However:

The author's methodology is educational and proprietary

Specific data aggregation, analysis, and scoring techniques are NOT disclosed in this book

Readers are taught to access federal data directly and interpret it independently

The author does NOT guarantee that this approach will produce results comparable to professional risk modeling services

No Substitute for Professional Services:

This book is NOT intended to replace:

Professional property inspections or engineering assessments

Insurance underwriting analysis or actuarial modeling

Real estate appraisals or market valuations

Legal advice about disclosure, liability, or contract terms

Financial planning or investment advisory services

Case Studies, Examples, and Composite Scenarios

Educational Illustrations

The personal stories, case studies, examples, statistics, and scenarios presented in this book are based on documented patterns from:

Court records and legal filings (publicly available case law)

Insurance industry data and claims statistics

Real estate transaction data and market trends

News reports, media coverage, and consumer complaints

Federal disaster declarations and damage assessments

However:

Names, locations, and specific details may be modified, composited, or anonymized to protect privacy

Dollar amounts, timelines, and outcomes represent typical ranges but will vary significantly by location, property characteristics, and individual circumstances

Examples are illustrative and should NOT be interpreted as predictions, promises, or guarantees of similar results

Your specific situation may differ materially from any example presented in this book

No Specific Properties Identified:

This book does NOT identify, evaluate, or make recommendations about specific properties, addresses, or listings. All examples are generalized educational illustrations.

Acknowledgment and Agreement

Binding Terms

By continuing to read and use this book, you acknowledge that you have read, understood, and agree to this disclaimer in its entirety. You further acknowledge and agree that:

Verification Responsibility: You will independently verify all information with current federal databases, licensed professionals, insurance carriers, and local authorities before making any property-related decisions.

Professional Consultation Required: You will consult appropriate licensed professionals (real estate attorneys, agents, inspectors, insurance agents, financial advisors) before purchasing property, signing contracts, or making financial commitments.

Data Currency Understanding: You understand that laws, regulations, federal data, insurance markets, and risk assessments change over time, and information in this book may become outdated.

Risk Acceptance: You accept full responsibility for your property purchasing decisions and their outcomes, understanding that all properties carry risk.

Probabilistic Nature: You understand that forward-looking projections and risk models are probabilistic, not guaranteed, and subject to uncertainty and revision.

Insurance Limitation: You understand that the author provides NO insurance advice and that actual insurance availability and pricing must be verified with licensed insurance professionals.

No Guarantees: You understand that following this book's guidance does NOT guarantee favorable outcomes, cost savings, risk avoidance, or transaction success.

Industry Context: You understand that comprehensive risk transparency may encounter resistance from industry stakeholders with different incentives.

Sole Reliance Prohibited: You will NOT rely solely on this book for real estate, legal, financial, insurance, or risk assessment advice.

Liability Waiver: You release the author, publisher, and affiliated entities from all liability for any loss, damage, or adverse outcome arising from use of this book.

AI-Assisted Content Development

This book was developed using AI writing tools to accelerate content creation and improve clarity. The author designed all analytical frameworks, chapter structures, data methodologies, and strategic guidance. AI tools assisted with drafting, organization, and explanation of complex concepts, but did not originate the core strategies, provide professional opinions, or make recommendations about specific properties or transactions.

All content was reviewed, edited, fact-checked, and approved by the author. The perspectives, risk assessment frameworks, and strategic recommendations reflect the author's judgment and interpretation of federal data sources and market research.

This disclosure does not alter the terms of this legal disclaimer. The book remains educational content only, not professional advice, and all liability limitations stated above continue to apply in full.

Questions, Concerns, or Additional Information

Resources for Readers

If you have questions about property risk analysis methodologies, federal database access, or educational resources, you may explore:

HomeDataReports.com — Comprehensive property intelligence reports aggregating federal data sources

PropertyRiskReports.com — Property risk analysis tools and educational resources

These platforms are owned by the author and provide property risk analysis services. They are NOT substitutes for professional advice from licensed real estate, insurance, legal, or financial professionals.

Final Statement

This disclaimer applies to both the Standard Edition and Expanded Edition of this book.

By proceeding past this disclaimer, you accept these terms and agree to use this book solely for educational purposes while seeking appropriate professional guidance for all property-related decisions.

The author believes in transparency, consumer empowerment, and informed decision-making. This book provides educational tools—but YOU remain solely responsible for how you use them.

Publication Date: December 2025

Author: Damian Martinez

Edition: [Standard Edition / Expanded Edition]

For publisher information, see the copyright page.

This disclaimer is designed to provide maximum legal protection while maintaining educational value. It addresses known industry disputes, regulatory uncertainty, data limitations, and consumer responsibility. Readers are strongly encouraged to consult licensed professionals before making any property-related decisions.

Introduction

Welcome friend to an amazing journey you're about to dive into! I'm am SUPER EXCITED that you picked up this book!

Not because I think you're about to make a terrible mistake (you're probably not). Not because I want to scare you away from buying a home (I definitely don't). But because you're about to learn something most homebuyers never discover until it's too late: **the data that matters most isn't in the listing photos or the home inspection report.**

It's hiding in plain sight—in federal databases, government websites, and public records that have been freely available for years. Most buyers just don't know where to look or what to do with the information once they find it.

That's where this book comes in.

Why I Wrote This Book:

Back in 2017, I became a licensed real estate agent. I thought I'd help people find their dream homes, negotiate great deals, and build a career in an industry I found fascinating.

And I did help people. But I also watched them make decisions that kept me up at night.

I watched buyers fall in love with a house during a showing, make an offer that same afternoon, and discover **after closing** that the property sat in a flood zone with $4,000 annual insurance premiums they hadn't budgeted for.

I watched buyers trust seller disclosures that said "no known issues," only to find out—months later—that the home sat a mile from an EPA Superfund site, or in an area with documented sinkhole activity, or directly in the path of projected wildfire expansion zones.

I watched smart, educated people make one of the biggest financial decisions of their lives based on incomplete information—not because they were careless, but because **no one told them what data existed or how to access it.**

By 2019, I'd left the real estate industry. Not because I didn't care about helping people buy homes—but because I realized the traditional process was broken. Buyers needed tools, not just representation. They needed **information**, not just opinions.

In 2020, I bought my own home. But I didn't buy it the traditional way. I pulled FEMA flood maps. I checked NOAA sea-level projections. I reviewed EPA environmental records within a three-mile radius. I got insurance quotes **before** making an offer. I calculated

30-year cost-of-ownership scenarios based on real data, not assumptions.

And I made an informed decision. Not a perfect one—there's no such thing—but an **informed** one. I knew exactly what I was buying, what risks I was accepting, and what costs I'd face over the long term.

After that, friends started asking for help. Then colleagues. Then friends of friends. I'd spend hours walking people through FEMA maps, explaining what "Zone AE" meant, showing them how to interpret EPA Superfund distances, teaching them how to get accurate insurance quotes before falling in love with a property.

It worked. People saved tens of thousands of dollars. They negotiated better. They avoided properties with risks they weren't willing to accept. They bought homes with full awareness and confidence.

But I wanted to make a bigger impact.

So I built **HomeDataReports.com**—a platform designed to aggregate federal data from 10+ government sources (FEMA, NOAA, USGS, EPA, Census, and more) into comprehensive property intelligence reports for any address in the United States. Today, we're working toward helping tens of thousands of property buyers every month across the country through HomeDataReports.com and our affiliated websites.

But I realized something: not everyone needs a full report for every property they're considering. Sometimes, people just need to **understand the process**. They need to know **what questions to ask, where to look, and how to interpret what they find.**

That's why I wrote this book.

<u>What This Book Is (And Isn't):</u>

This book is **not** going to tell you to avoid buying a home.

It's not going to scare you away from flood zones, wildfire areas, earthquake regions, or neighborhoods near environmental concerns.

Why? Because **every home has risks.** A house in a quiet suburban neighborhood with no flood zone, no wildfire threat, and no seismic activity still has risks—foundation issues, roof problems, aging systems, market downturns, or any of a hundred other variables.

The goal isn't to find a risk-free property. **The goal is to understand the specific risks of the property you're considering—and decide whether those are risks you're willing and able to manage.**

A flood zone might be a dealbreaker for one family but perfectly acceptable to another who's budgeted for flood insurance and wants that specific location. A wildfire-prone area might be off-limits for some buyers but an ideal choice for others who are committed to proper mitigation and love the mountain views.

This book exists to help you make informed, data-driven decisions—not to make decisions for you.

<u>How This Book Works:</u>

Over the next 14 chapters, I'm going to walk you through the exact process I use to research property risk—the same system that's helped thousands of buyers make smarter decisions.

You'll learn:

How to access and interpret federal flood maps (Chapter 2)

What hurricanes, storm surge, and coastal risks really mean for your property (Chapter 3)

How to evaluate earthquake zones and understand seismic hazard data (Chapter 4)

Where wildfires are expanding and how to assess fire risk (Chapter 5)

What environmental contamination data you need to check—and how close is too close (Chapter 6)

How climate change projections affect long-term property values (Chapter 7)

What your insurance company knows that you don't—and how to get ahead of coverage gaps (Chapters 8-9)

How to use all this data to negotiate better, avoid surprises, and make confident decisions (Chapters 10-14)

Some of this content may not apply to where you live. If you're buying in Arizona, the hurricane chapter won't be relevant. If you're in Kansas, you can skim the wildfire section. But even if a chapter doesn't apply to **your** property search, it might help a friend, family member, or colleague in another part of the country—so I'd still recommend reading it.

Real estate is one of those industries where knowledge compounds. The more you understand, the better decisions you make—not just on this purchase, but on future investments, refinancing decisions, insurance reviews, and strategic planning over the decades you'll own your home.

A Quick Note on Tone:

I wrote this book the way I'd explain property risk to a friend over coffee. I'm not a lawyer, so you won't find legal jargon. I'm not an academic, so you won't find endless citations and footnotes. I'm a guy who spent years figuring out how to make federal data **useful** instead of overwhelming—and I'm going to share that process with you in plain English.

You'll find real examples, real numbers, and real strategies. You'll also find a few warnings, some frustration about how broken the disclosure system is, and occasional references to the absurdity of expecting buyers to navigate all this on their own with zero guidance.

But mostly, you'll find **practical, actionable information** you can use tomorrow when you start researching properties.

Let's Get Started:

By the time you finish this book, you'll know more about property risk analysis than 95% of homebuyers. You'll know where to look, what to ask, and how to use federal data to protect yourself from six-figure surprises.

You'll make better offers. You'll negotiate with confidence. You'll avoid properties with risks you're not willing to accept. And when you do find the right home—one where you understand and accept the risks—you'll close with clarity, not anxiety.

That's the goal. That's why I wrote this. And I'm genuinely glad you're here.

Let's dive in.

— **Damian Martinez**

Founder, HomeDataReports.com

Contents

1. The $300K to $800K+ Blind Spot 1
2. What Your Home Inspection Misses 12
3. The Overlooked Federal Data Systems 19
4. Flood & Water Risks 32
5. Hurricane Risk — The $24,000 Surprise 39
6. Earthquake & Seismic Risks: The National Blind Spot 46
7. Wildfire Risks 53
8. Environmental Hazards 61
9. Climate Change Impacts 69
10. Demographic & Crime Data 77
11. Pulling It All Together 91
12. Your Pre-Offer Checklist 99
13. Turning Data Into Negotiation Power 107
14. Beyond Closing Day — Annual Monitoring & Long-Term Strategy 116
15. Final Thoughts 125
16. Appendix: Essential Resources & References 131
17. Glossary of Terms 137
18. About the Author 143
19. Your Next Step: Turn Knowledge Into Action 144

Chapter 1

The $300K to $800K+ Blind Spot

The Dream That Became a Nightmare

It started like every homebuyer's dream.

Sarah and Daniel walked through a beautiful house on a quiet street. Two kids, stable jobs, ready to put down roots. The price was $475,000. They signed the papers, got the keys, and started planning backyard barbecues.

One month later, their insurance company called.

"We can't insure your home."

Sarah thought it was a mistake. The house was practically new. Great neighborhood. Clean inspection report. How could this happen?

Then the truth came out. **The ground beneath their house had partially collapsed years ago.** A sinkhole event. The previous owners took a $155,000 insurance settlement in 2010, patched the cracks, painted over the evidence, and sold the house quietly. On paper, the disclosure said "no known sinkhole issues."

But the federal geological data told a different story.

Sarah and Daniel had just invested nearly half a million dollars—not just money, but their family's future. Instead of security, they got stress. Instead of building equity, they got a house they couldn't insure, couldn't sell, and might not be safe to live in.

Sarah and Daniel invested nearly half a million dollars—not just money, but their family's future. Instead of security, they got a house they couldn't insure, couldn't sell, and might not be safe to live in.

They're not alone.

Across the country, homebuyers are discovering major problems after closing. Construction defects costing $400,000+ to repair. Foundations sinking into underground water. Wildfire smoke leaving toxic ash. Flood zones that slash resale value by $100,000 or more.

Here's what makes it worse: **all of this information was available before they bought.** Federal agencies track it. Geological surveys document it. Environmental databases record it. But nobody in the traditional home-buying process actually checks this data.

This chapter is about closing that gap before it costs you everything.

What Your Real Estate Team Never Checks

When you buy a house, you hire a team of professionals. A real estate agent shows you the property and handles negotiations. A home inspector checks the structure, roof, plumbing, and electrical systems. An appraiser confirms the price matches the market.

Here's what none of them check: long-term federal risk data.

The Traditional Process Covers What You See Today

Your agent focuses on what makes the house appealing—layout, finishes, neighborhood comparables. Your inspector looks at what's physically present—foundation cracks, roof condition, HVAC function. Your appraiser verifies the price matches similar properties sold recently.

All of this answers one question: **Is the house in good condition right now?**

Nobody asks: What hazards has this property experienced in the past? What risks is it exposed to in the future? What does the federal government know about this location that I don't?

> **KEY TAKEAWAY**
>
> Your real estate team checks today's condition. Federal data reveals tomorrow's risks. The professionals in your corner aren't trained to look at government hazard databases—it's just not part of the standard process.

Why This Gap Exists

The gap exists because **disclosure laws are weak**. In many states, sellers only have to disclose what they personally know. If the previous owner experienced a problem but never told them, they technically don't "know" about it. If an issue happened 15 years ago and was quietly repaired, it might not be on their radar at all.

Real estate agents aren't required to pull federal hazard data. Home inspectors check the current physical condition—they're not geological experts or environmental scientists. Appraisers compare sale prices—they're not researching government databases for historical flood events or EPA contamination sites.

The professionals in your corner aren't trained to look at this information. It's not their fault. It's just not part of the standard process.

And that's the problem.

REAL STORY: The $435,936 Defect

Joseph and Dunia Sabga bought a new home in Florida in 2017. During the final walkthrough before closing, they documented construction defects on a punch list. The builder agreed to fix everything within 30 days.

The builder never did.

By 2022, the repair costs had grown to **$322,916**. By trial in 2023, inflation pushed costs to **$435,936**. The trial court awarded them damages—but on appeal, the judgment was reversed on a technicality. The Sabgas ended up with nothing. No recovery. No repairs. Just a defective house and years of legal stress.

Or consider Adam and Victoria Cooper in Spring Hill, Florida. They bought their dream home only to discover it sat on top of a massive sinkhole. Despite the danger, they couldn't easily walk away. By the time they uncovered the full extent of the problem, they'd already invested everything.

These aren't rare cases. **They're happening every single day.**

The difference between a smart purchase and a financial disaster often comes down to one thing: **did you check the federal data before you signed?**

"The difference between a smart purchase and a financial disaster often comes down to one thing: did you check the federal data before you signed?"

How Federal Data Closes the Gap

Here's the good news: **all of this information is publicly available.**

The federal government tracks property risks through multiple agencies:

- **FEMA** (Federal Emergency Management Agency) documents flood zones, disaster history, and claims data
- **NOAA** (National Oceanic and Atmospheric Administration) tracks climate patterns, storm surge zones, and sea-level rise

- **USGS** (United States Geological Survey) maps earthquake zones, sinkholes, landslides, and ground stability
- **EPA** (Environmental Protection Agency) monitors contamination sites, toxic spills, and air quality hazards
- **Census Bureau** provides demographic data that reveals shifting neighborhood dynamics

This isn't hidden information. It's not locked behind paywalls or insider connections. It's federal data—paid for by your tax dollars—sitting in government databases waiting to be accessed.

The problem is that nobody in the traditional home-buying process pulls it for you.

Why This Matters More Now Than Ever

According to recent surveys, **80% of homebuyers now consider climate risk** when purchasing a property. People are waking up to the fact that a house isn't just about square footage and granite countertops. It's about long-term safety and financial stability.

But here's the disconnect: buyers say they care about risk, yet they're still not accessing the data that reveals it. They rely on listing descriptions that say "no flood risk" when FEMA maps tell a different story. They trust sellers who claim "no issues" when geological records show prior sinkhole activity.

You can't make informed decisions with incomplete information.

> *"Federal data isn't hidden—it's paid for by your tax dollars and sitting in government databases. The problem is nobody in the traditional home-buying process pulls it for you."*

What Federal Data Actually Tells You

When you run a property through federal databases, here's what you learn:

- **Has this property ever flooded?** Not just whether it's in a flood zone—but whether FEMA has paid out claims here before.
- **Is the ground stable?** Geological surveys reveal sinkhole-prone areas, soil subsidence, and underground water issues.

- **Are there environmental hazards nearby?** EPA data shows contamination sites, toxic spills, and air quality problems within a searchable radius.
- **What's the long-term climate outlook?** NOAA projections show how sea-level rise, storm intensity, and temperature changes will impact this location over 30 years.
- **Is this area getting riskier or safer?** Trends in disaster declarations and insurance payouts reveal whether risks are increasing.

This isn't about fear-mongering. It's about **replacing guesswork with facts.**

Warning Signs You're Buying Blind

Most homebuyers don't realize they're missing critical information until it's too late. Here are the red flags that should trigger an immediate deep dive into federal risk data:

⚠ RED FLAG #1: "No Flood Risk" on the Listing

Sellers and agents often label properties as "not in a flood zone" based on outdated maps or incorrect interpretation. FEMA updates flood zones regularly. A house that wasn't in a flood zone five years ago might be today.

Real example: Multiple buyers in North Carolina purchased homes labeled "no flood risk" only to be devastated by Hurricane Helene in 2024. Many had no flood insurance because they trusted the listing description. Federal data would have shown prior flood events in those areas.

⚠ RED FLAG #2: Foundation or Structural "Repairs" in Disclosure

If the seller discloses that foundation work or structural repairs were done, dig deeper. What caused the problem in the first place? Was it a one-time issue or an ongoing geological problem?

USGS geological surveys can reveal if the property sits in a zone with soil subsidence, underground water movement, or sinkhole activity. A "fixed" foundation might just be a temporary patch on a permanent problem.

⚠ RED FLAG #3: "Great Deal" in a High-Risk Area

If a property is priced significantly below comparable homes in the area, there's usually a reason. Sometimes it's cosmetic. Other times, it's because informed buyers have already passed on it after running the data.

Before you jump on a bargain, check federal databases. That "great price" might reflect risks the seller knows about but isn't required to disclose.

⚠ **RED FLAG #4: Insurance Quotes That Seem High**

If you get an insurance quote and the premium is shockingly high—or worse, if multiple carriers decline to insure the property—that's a massive red flag.

Insurance companies use federal hazard data to assess risk. If they're pricing the property as high-risk or refusing coverage, they've already done the research you should have done before making an offer.

How to Buy With Intelligence: A Step-by-Step Framework

Now that you understand **why** federal data matters and **what** it reveals, let's talk about **when** and **how** to use it in your home-buying process.

The good news: you don't need to be an expert. You just need to access the right information at the right time.

Before You Make an Offer

☐ **ACTION STEP 1:** Run a comprehensive property intelligence report on any house you're seriously considering.

This should happen **before** you make an offer. Not after. Not during the inspection period. Before.

Why? Because once you're emotionally invested and money is on the line, it's psychologically harder to walk away. Get the facts first.

☐ **ACTION STEP 2:** Review the report with a critical eye.

Look for:

- Flood zone classification and historical claims
- Environmental hazards within 1-3 miles
- Geological stability issues
- Long-term climate projections

Don't dismiss red flags. If something looks concerning, it probably is.

☐ **ACTION STEP 3:** Use the data to negotiate.

If the report reveals risks, you now have leverage. Negotiate a lower price, request seller concessions for mitigation (like flood barriers or soil testing), or walk away entirely before you're in too deep.

During the Inspection Period

☐ **ACTION STEP 4:** Share the risk data with your home inspector.

Give your inspector the property report so they can focus their physical inspection on areas flagged by federal data. If there's a history of water intrusion, they'll know to look harder at drainage systems and foundation integrity.

☐ **ACTION STEP 5:** Decide with eyes wide open.

Not every risk is a dealbreaker. A flood zone might be fine if you're comfortable with the insurance cost and have a mitigation plan. The point isn't to avoid all risk—it's to **know what you're accepting and price it accordingly.**

"This book isn't about scaring you away from homes. It's about giving you the information to make decisions that are right for YOU."

Before Closing (Final Week)

☐ **ACTION STEP 6:** Run a final verification check.

Federal databases are updated regularly. Make sure no new hazard declarations, flood map changes, or environmental alerts were issued between your initial check and closing day.

☐ **ACTION STEP 7:** Lock in insurance with accurate premiums.

Confirm your insurance is approved and reflects the true risk profile. No surprises after closing.

☐ **ACTION STEP 8:** Proceed only if you're comfortable.

At this stage, you should have complete information. If something feels off, you still have time to walk away.

What You Gain When You Buy With Intelligence

Let me show you what this looks like in practice.

SUCCESS STORY: Sarah and Mike's $30,000+ Savings

Sarah and Mike were about to make an offer on a $425,000 home in Tampa. Before they did, they ran a comprehensive property intelligence report.

The report revealed two major issues:

1. **The house sat in a moderate-risk flood zone** that wasn't clearly disclosed on the listing.

2. **It was only 0.3 miles from an active EPA Superfund cleanup site**—a toxic contamination area being actively monitored by the government.

Armed with this information, they requested real insurance quotes. The flood premium came back at **$450 per month**—far higher than the $150/month typical for a standard homeowners policy.

Instead of walking away, Sarah and Mike used the data to negotiate. They went back to the seller with the federal reports and insurance quotes in hand.

The seller agreed to:

- Reduce the purchase price by **$25,000**
- Cover the cost of an elevation certificate (useful for future insurance and resale)
- Provide documentation of mitigation efforts already completed

Over five years, Sarah and Mike estimate they saved more than **$30,000** compared to what they would have paid without this knowledge.

More importantly, they bought with confidence. They knew exactly what they were getting into. The risks were factored into the price. Their insurance was locked in. No surprises.

THE REAL COST OF BUYING BLIND

WITHOUT PROPERTY DATA:

- Purchase price: $425,000
- Hidden flood insurance: +$450/month ($27,000 over 5 years)
- Resale value hit: -$100,000
- **TOTAL LOSS: $127,000+**

WITH PROPERTY DATA:

- Negotiated price: $400,000
- Known flood costs: $450/month (budgeted)
- Informed decision: Priceless
- **SAVINGS: $25,000+ plus peace of mind**

The Real Reward: Peace of Mind

Buying a home is the largest financial decision most people ever make. You're not just buying a structure—you're buying security for your family, a place to build memories, and hopefully a sound financial investment.

When you buy with intelligence, you get:

- **Negotiating power** to lower the price or get seller concessions
- **Insurance certainty** so you're not scrambling after closing
- **Resale protection** because future buyers will care about these risks too
- **Peace of mind** knowing you made a decision based on facts, not hope

You don't have to be an expert in geology, environmental science, or climate modeling. You just need to access the data that experts use—and factor it into your decision **before** you sign the papers.

"A flood zone might be a dealbreaker for one family but perfectly acceptable to another who's budgeted for flood insurance. What matters is that you KNOW before you buy—not discover it after closing."

Chapter 1 Recap

Here's what you learned:

✓ The traditional home-buying process checks today's physical condition—but misses long-term federal risk data

✓ Federal agencies (FEMA, NOAA, USGS, EPA) track property hazards that your real estate team never checks

✓ Disclosure laws are weak—sellers only have to tell you what they personally know

✓ 80% of homebuyers care about climate risk, but most still don't access the data that reveals it

✓ Running property intelligence reports BEFORE making an offer gives you negotiating power and peace of mind

✓ The goal isn't to avoid all risk—it's to know what you're accepting and price it accordingly

Now that you understand **why** property intelligence matters and **what** it can do for you, it's time to dig deeper.

In the next chapter, we'll break down exactly what your standard home inspection misses—and why combining a physical inspection with data-driven risk analysis gives you the complete picture before you commit.

Because buying a home isn't just about checking for roof leaks and faulty wiring. It's about understanding the invisible risks that could cost you hundreds of thousands of dollars down the road.

Chapter Resources

Feel free to skip ahead if you'd like to continue reading.

Ready to See What You've Been Missing?

You just learned about the blind spots that cost buyers hundreds of thousands of dollars. Now it's time to eliminate those blind spots for your own property search.

Create a free account at **HomeDataReports.com** and get your first Essential Report completely free when you sign up. Think of it as a comprehensive property intelligence report—like a detailed vehicle history report, but for homes—pulling data from 10+ federal sources (FEMA, NOAA, USGS, EPA, and more) into a single, easy-to-read analysis.

Test our proprietary risk calculator to see how any U.S. property scores across flood, wildfire, earthquake, environmental, and climate risks. Download our free Chrome extension to instantly check properties while browsing Zillow, Redfin, or Realtor.com. And if you found this chapter eye-opening, share it with friends, family, or your real estate agent—they'll thank you for it.

Are you a realtor, lender, home inspector, or insurance agent? Join our partner referral program and help your clients make informed decisions while building a new revenue stream for your business.

Chapter 2

What Your Home Inspection Misses

You signed the closing papers with confidence. The inspection came back clean. "Everything checked out," the inspector said—foundation solid, roof good, plumbing safe, all systems functional.

Flash forward a few seasons. A routine news alert about rising flood zones. Wildfire smoke filling the sky. An insurance renewal letter with a premium that doubled overnight. That safe investment suddenly carried risks you never saw coming.

Not because anything failed. The inspector was honest. The structure was sound.

The problem was what the inspection never tested.

A standard home inspection only covers what's visible and accessible. It can't predict what's coming—or what's already hidden.

The Gap Nobody Talks About

Here's what most buyers don't realize: a home inspection checks if the house works today. It doesn't check if the location is safe tomorrow.

Your $400-500 inspection covers visible systems—foundation, roof, plumbing, electrical, HVAC. The inspector walks through, takes notes, and delivers a report on what they can see in that moment.

But here's what it doesn't cover:

> **□ RED FLAG #1: Your inspection won't reveal flood zones, wildfire risk, or earthquake zones. These aren't structural issues—they're location-based threats requiring different data sources.**

Standard inspections exclude environmental hazards unless specifically requested. No radon testing, soil contamination analysis, mold detection, underground tank checks, or toxic waste screening. Nothing about future insurability, climate risk, or long-term property value threats.

A "clean" inspection does NOT equal a "safe" property when it comes to environmental risk, flood zones, or climate factors.

Home inspectors aren't hiding anything—they operate within defined professional standards. They can't tear open walls, dig up yards, or research federal flood maps. That's outside their scope.

The problem is buyer expectations. "Inspection contingency" sounds comprehensive. A clean report feels conclusive. But invisible threats easily slip through.

Inspections answer "Is the house sound?" Property intelligence answers "Is the location sound?" You need both.

The Disclosure Loophole

Disclosure laws vary wildly by state. California requires detailed hazard disclosures. Texas allows sellers to skip them entirely. Twenty-nine states don't require flood zone disclosure at all.

Even in strict states, sellers only disclose what they know. Never tested for radon? Don't know about soil contamination? Legally, they don't have to tell you.

□ RED FLAG #2: In 29 states, sellers can hide previous flood damage. You won't know until the next storm hits.

The Two-Layer Approach

When you buy a home, you're asking two different questions:

1. **Is the house structurally sound?** (Inspection answers this)

2. **Is the location safe long-term?** (Property intelligence answers this)

Most buyers only ask the first question. That's the gap.

□ **ACTION STEP 1:** Run a property intelligence report BEFORE scheduling your inspection. Takes 3 minutes, often free. You need location data FIRST.

Layer 1: Property Intelligence (Run First)

These reports pull federal data—FEMA flood maps, NOAA climate data, USGS earthquake risk, EPA environmental records. They reveal:

- Flood zones and historical flooding
- Wildfire risk scores
- Earthquake fault lines
- Environmental hazards (contaminated soil, radon)
- Climate projections
- Insurance cost trends

□ **ACTION STEP 2:** Review the report carefully. Look for red flags that would make you reconsider—or negotiate mitigation.

Layer 2: Standard Inspection (Run Second, Strategically)

Once you understand location risks, schedule your inspection. Now you're not blind—you can direct the inspector to check risk-related vulnerabilities.

Wildfire risk? Ask about roof materials, vegetation clearance, drainage. Flood risk? Request focus on foundation waterproofing, sump pumps, basement conditions.

Run property intelligence BEFORE the inspection. It turns a generic walk-through into a targeted risk assessment.

□ **ACTION STEP 3:** Use both reports during negotiations. If intelligence reveals risk AND inspection finds vulnerabilities, you have leverage for repairs, credits, or mitigation.

Warning Signs You're Missing Critical Information

□ RED FLAG #3: Your agent says "the inspection will cover everything." No, it won't. If they're not discussing location risks separately, they're uninformed or hoping you won't ask.

□ RED FLAG #4: You're buying in a weak disclosure state (Florida, Texas, Alabama) and the seller's disclosure is brief. They might be legally compliant while hiding major risks.

□ RED FLAG #5: Your insurance quote comes back significantly higher than expected—or excludes flood/wildfire coverage. By then you're already under contract.

□ **ACTION STEP 4:** Research flood zones, wildfire maps, and environmental hazards BEFORE making an offer. Waiting until after contract means you've already committed emotionally.

The time to discover your dream home is in a flood zone is BEFORE you make an offer—not after you've fallen in love with the kitchen.

Your Step-by-Step Plan

□ **ACTION STEP 5:** Before making offers, run basic property intelligence on every home you're seriously considering. Many services offer free essential reports.

□ **ACTION STEP 6:** Once under contract, upgrade to comprehensive property intelligence ($10-20) that includes climate projections and detailed risk analysis.

□ **ACTION STEP 7:** Schedule your inspection AFTER reviewing property intelligence. Share findings with your inspector for targeted examination.

□ **ACTION STEP 8:** Use both reports during negotiations. Demand seller credits, require mitigation, or walk away if risks are too high.

Case Study: The $15,000 Negotiation

Sarah and Mike ran a property intelligence report before their inspection on a Fort Collins home. It flagged high wildfire risk.

They asked their inspector to focus on fire vulnerabilities. He found aging cedar shake roof, overhanging branches, accumulated debris, and no defensible space clearing.

They negotiated:

- $12,000 credit for fire-resistant roof
- $3,000 credit for vegetation clearing
- Seller-paid wildfire insurance (first year)

Total savings: $15,000 immediate, plus thousands annually in reduced premiums.

They bought the home they loved—with full knowledge and proper mitigation.

What You Gain

When you run both layers, you get clarity, confidence, and leverage. You're not just buying walls and a roof—you're buying a place to build your life.

This book isn't about scaring you away from homes. It's about giving you information to make decisions right for YOU. What matters is that you KNOW before you buy.

The two-layer approach transforms you from a passive buyer into an informed decision-maker who understands exactly what you're buying and what risks you're accepting.

□ **FINAL ACTION:** Commit to running property intelligence on EVERY property you seriously consider. Make it routine. Takes 3 minutes, could save you $50,000+.

Chapter 2 Key Takeaways

□ Standard inspections only check if the house works today—not if location is safe tomorrow

□ Inspections exclude environmental hazards, flood zones, wildfire risk, and climate projections unless requested

□ 29 states don't require flood zone disclosure—disclosure laws vary wildly

□ Two-layer approach: Property intelligence FIRST, then targeted inspection

□ Federal data (FEMA, NOAA, USGS, EPA) reveals risks invisible to inspectors

□ Both reports together give negotiating leverage—demand credits or walk away

□ Clean inspection ≠ safe property—you need structural AND location intelligence

Now that you understand what inspections miss—and how property intelligence fills those gaps—the next step is seeing where that intelligence comes from.

In Chapter 3, I'll walk you through the federal databases, climate maps, and public records most buyers never know exist—but which can make or break your decision.

Let's decode the data so you can shop with your eyes open.

Chapter 3

The Overlooked Federal Data Systems

The offer was almost ready.

A young couple had been searching for months, and they finally found a home that checked all the boxes: a three-bedroom property listed for $380,000 in a quiet neighborhood, close to work, recently updated, and within their budget. Their realtor encouraged them to move quickly, reminding them that similar homes were receiving multiple offers within days.

Excited, they called a close friend to share the news—someone who happened to work in emergency management at FEMA. After listening, their friend asked a single question that changed everything:

"Did you check the flood maps?"

They hadn't. They assumed their realtor or the listing platform would highlight anything important. Still, out of caution, they went to the FEMA Flood Map Service Center, typed in the property address, and waited as the map loaded.

What appeared next made their stomachs sink.

"One federal database search saved them $90,000 over 30 years. The data was free. They just didn't know it existed."

The home sat directly inside an AE flood zone, a high-risk category that often requires elevated insurance premiums and additional building standards. They dug deeper and reached out to an insurance agent.

The quote came back at **$4,200 per year**.

They compared it to a similar property in a low-risk zone they had toured earlier, where the estimated premium was closer to **$1,200 per year**. That difference—**an extra $3,000**

every year—added up to **$90,000 over a 30-year mortgage**. And that number didn't include potential future increases due to climate trends or new federal mapping updates.

Suddenly, the "dream home" looked very different.

They walked away from the offer, continued their search, and found another property just a few streets over—similar layout, similar price—but located outside the high-risk zone. Insurance: **less than a third of the cost**. Same neighborhood, same schools, same commute... radically different long-term financial outcome.

And here's the most surprising part:

The flood data was publicly available the entire time. It wasn't hidden behind paywalls, subscription services, or exclusive industry tools. Anyone with an internet connection could access it in under five minutes. The couple just didn't know where to look.

That's the reality for millions of American homebuyers every year. The most powerful property intelligence in the country sits in plain sight—maintained by seven federal agencies, updated regularly, completely free—yet most people never use it.

This chapter changes that.

Most Buyers Have No Idea This Exists

Here's what most people assume when shopping for a home:

"If something's seriously wrong with a property, someone will tell me about it."

That "someone" could be the seller, the realtor, the inspector, or the listing platform. The assumption is simple: if flooding is a concern, wildfire risk is increasing, or a Superfund site sits nearby, surely it would come up during the process.

But that's not how disclosure works.

> **□ RED FLAG #1: Sellers are only required to disclose what they know—and in many states, that's surprisingly little.**

In over half of U.S. states, sellers have no legal obligation to inform buyers about flood risk. They don't have to mention that insurance premiums tripled after the last storm season. They don't have to explain that a nearby creek has overflowed three times in five years. Unless they experienced flood damage themselves or know about it firsthand, they simply don't disclose it.

Realtors operate under the same constraints. If the seller doesn't mention it, the realtor may not know about it either. And even when they do know, they're not obligated to provide comprehensive risk analysis—they're there to facilitate the transaction, not conduct environmental assessments.

Home inspectors check for structural issues, electrical problems, plumbing concerns, and visible defects. But they don't analyze federal databases. They don't review FEMA flood zones or EPA Superfund registries. Their job is to evaluate what's physically present—not what federal agencies have documented.

> *"The federal government already collected the data. They mapped the risks. They published the findings. Most buyers just never look."*

That leaves one group responsible for finding this information: **you**.

And the truth is, most buyers don't even know these databases exist. They assume private companies like Zillow or Redfin provide comprehensive risk intelligence. But these platforms typically offer surface-level summaries—simplified scores that don't reflect the full depth of federal data.

Here's what federal agencies actually provide:

- **FEMA** maintains flood insurance rate maps showing every high-risk zone nationwide
- **USGS** tracks earthquakes, landslides, and soil stability
- **EPA** monitors Superfund sites, air quality, and radon exposure
- **NOAA** analyzes climate trends, wildfire risk, and severe weather patterns
- **USDA** surveys soil quality and agricultural land use
- **FBI** publishes detailed crime statistics for every community
- **Census Bureau** tracks demographics, housing trends, and economic indicators

This isn't private market research. This is **authoritative federal data**, collected by agencies with legal mandates to track exactly these kinds of risks. It's not opinion-based. It's not speculative. It's documented evidence compiled by government scientists, geologists, environmental engineers, and law enforcement agencies.

> The most comprehensive property risk data in America is free and publicly accessible—but only if you know where to find it.

How Federal Data Actually Works

Federal agencies don't collect property data to help homebuyers make better decisions. That's not their mission. They collect it because Congress mandated them to track specific risks, respond to disasters, protect public health, and monitor national trends.

But here's the fortunate side effect: **all of that data becomes publicly accessible under federal transparency laws.**

Let's break down how each database works and why it matters.

FEMA — National Flood Insurance Program (NFIP)

FEMA creates and maintains Flood Insurance Rate Maps (FIRMs) for every community participating in the National Flood Insurance Program. These maps identify flood zones, categorize risk levels, and establish insurance requirements.

What you get:

- Official flood zone designation (A, AE, X, etc.)
- Historical flood event data
- Base flood elevation requirements
- Insurance rate structures

Why it matters: Flood insurance can cost anywhere from $500 to $5,000+ per year depending on your zone. Knowing this before you buy means you can budget accurately—or walk away if the cost doesn't make sense.

> ☐ Visit the FEMA Flood Map Service Center (msc.fema.gov) and enter every address you're seriously considering. Write down the flood zone designation and call an insurance agent for a quote **before** making an offer.

USGS — U.S. Geological Survey

USGS monitors seismic activity, landslides, sinkholes, soil stability, and groundwater conditions. Their earthquake hazard maps show probabilistic risk levels for every region, and their landslide susceptibility maps identify unstable terrain.

What you get:

- Earthquake probability projections
- Landslide risk assessments

- Soil composition data
- Groundwater availability

Why it matters: If you're buying in California, the Pacific Northwest, or other seismically active areas, understanding earthquake risk isn't optional—it's foundational. Insurance, retrofitting costs, and long-term property values all hinge on seismic stability.

"Federal data tells you what's underneath your property—not just what's on top of it."

EPA — Environmental Protection Agency

The EPA tracks environmental hazards that directly impact property values and public health. Their databases include Superfund sites (contaminated areas requiring federal cleanup), Toxic Release Inventory facilities, air quality monitoring stations, and radon exposure maps.

What you get:

- Superfund site proximity and contamination status
- Air quality index for your ZIP code
- Industrial pollutant releases nearby
- Radon risk levels

Why it matters: Living near a Superfund site can reduce property values by 10-25%. High radon levels require mitigation systems costing $800-$2,500. Poor air quality affects health outcomes and insurance rates. This data isn't about paranoia—it's about informed decision-making.

□ RED FLAG #2: EPA data updates when new contamination is discovered. A clean report today doesn't guarantee a clean report five years from now—but knowing the baseline matters.

NOAA — National Oceanic and Atmospheric Administration

NOAA analyzes climate trends, severe weather patterns, wildfire risk, and coastal hazards. Their climate data extends decades into the past and includes forward-looking projections based on historical trends.

What you get:

- Wildfire exposure ratings
- Hurricane frequency and intensity
- Drought and heat trend analysis
- Sea level rise projections for coastal areas

Why it matters: Climate risk isn't abstract—it's financial. Wildfire-prone areas see insurance premiums double or triple. Coastal properties face increasing flood risk and potential loss of insurability. NOAA's data shows you what's coming, not just what happened last year.

USDA — Natural Resources Conservation Service

The USDA maintains detailed soil surveys for agricultural and residential land use. These surveys identify soil types, drainage patterns, erosion risk, and load-bearing capacity.

What you get:

- Soil composition and stability
- Drainage characteristics
- Erosion susceptibility
- Agricultural productivity ratings

Why it matters: Soil matters more than most people realize. Expansive clay soils cause foundation cracks. Poor drainage creates flooding issues. Erosion undermines property boundaries. USDA data reveals these risks before they become expensive problems.

☐ Visit the USDA Web Soil Survey (websoilsurvey.nrcs.usda.gov) and generate a soil report for your property. Look specifically for drainage class, depth to water table, and corrosion potential.

FBI — Uniform Crime Reporting (UCR) Program

The FBI publishes crime statistics for cities and counties nationwide, including violent crime rates, property crime rates, and clearance rates (how often crimes are solved).

What you get:

- Violent crime rates per 100,000 residents
- Property crime trends over time
- Arrest and clearance statistics
- Comparison to state and national averages

Why it matters: Safety isn't subjective. FBI data shows you actual reported crime rates, not neighborhood rumors or outdated perceptions. This information affects property values, insurance costs, and resale prospects.

U.S. Census Bureau

The Census Bureau tracks demographics, income levels, housing statistics, and economic trends. Their American Community Survey updates annually, providing granular neighborhood data.

What you get:

- Median household income
- Educational attainment
- Home ownership rates
- Population growth or decline

Why it matters: Economic trends predict long-term property appreciation. Neighborhoods with rising incomes and stable populations tend to hold value better than areas experiencing decline. Census data reveals these patterns before they become obvious.

"Seven databases. Seven perspectives. One complete picture of what you're actually buying."

When to Walk Away (Or Renegotiate)

Federal data doesn't just inform decisions—it reveals deal-breakers. Here's what to watch for:

□ RED FLAG #3: If flood insurance costs more than 2% of the home's purchase price annually, you're looking at a property with significant long-term financial exposure.

FEMA Warning Signs:

- Property in AE, A, or V flood zones (high-risk designations)
- Multiple flood claims filed in the last 10 years
- Base flood elevation higher than the property's foundation

EPA Warning Signs:

- Superfund site within 1 mile (especially if "active remediation" status)
- Radon levels above 4 pCi/L
- Air quality consistently rated "Unhealthy for Sensitive Groups" or worse

NOAA Warning Signs:

- Wildfire risk rated "High" or "Very High" with increasing frequency trends
- Hurricane exposure in areas where insurers are withdrawing coverage
- Coastal properties with documented erosion or sea level rise concerns

USGS Warning Signs:

- Earthquake probability exceeding 10% in the next 50 years
- Landslide susceptibility rated "High" or higher
- Soil surveys showing "Very Poor" drainage or high shrink-swell potential

□ Create a simple spreadsheet with columns for each database and rows for each property you're considering. Mark any property with 2+ red flags for immediate elimination or aggressive negotiation.

Your Federal Data Checklist

Ready to use this data? Here's your step-by-step process:

□ **Step 1:** Make a list of every property you're seriously considering (3-5 addresses maximum to start).

□ **Step 2:** Set aside 45-60 minutes for each property. Yes, this takes time—but it's worth thousands of dollars.

□ **Step 3:** Visit each federal database in order:

1. FEMA Flood Maps (msc.fema.gov)
2. USGS Earthquake Hazards (earthquake.usgs.gov/hazards)
3. EPA EnviroFacts (enviro.epa.gov)
4. NOAA Climate Data (ncdc.noaa.gov)
5. USDA Web Soil Survey (websoilsurvey.nrcs.usda.gov)
6. FBI Crime Data Explorer (crime-data-explorer.fr.cloud.gov)
7. Census Bureau QuickFacts (census.gov/quickfacts)

□ **Step 4:** For each database, screenshot or save the key findings. Create a simple one-page summary per property.

□ **Step 5 (Optional):** If manually checking databases feels overwhelming, use an aggregation service like **Home Data Reports** to pull all seven sources into one comprehensive report. It costs less than a single dinner out and saves hours of research time.

"The data exists. The question isn't whether you should check it—it's how fast you want the answer."

What Happens When You Actually Use This

Let's look at two real outcomes.

Case Study 1: The Austin Researcher

A tech-savvy buyer from the Austin suburbs wasn't an investor, a developer, or a real estate professional—just someone who loved research and wanted to make a responsible purchase.

He found a home he liked and decided to spend an entire weekend reviewing every federal database covered in this chapter. One by one, he pulled the FEMA flood maps, USGS seismic data, EPA environmental reports, NOAA climate patterns, USDA soil surveys, FBI crime statistics, and Census demographics.

What he discovered changed everything.

The property sat in a **moderate flood risk zone**, according to FEMA. An **EPA Superfund site** was located just outside the neighborhood boundary. NOAA projections showed increasing **wildfire exposure** over the next decade due to regional drought patterns. None of this appeared in the listing. None of it came up in conversations with the seller. And none of it appeared in the clean home inspection.

Armed with documented federal evidence, he negotiated a **$35,000 price reduction**.

When the seller insisted the inspection found no issues, the buyer simply showed the official FEMA maps and EPA reports. There wasn't anything to debate—these weren't his opinions. They were authoritative U.S. government assessments. The seller agreed to the reduction, and the closing went smoothly.

Today, he still loves the home—but he also monitors these federal databases annually to track changes and prepare for long-term risk.

The lesson? Federal data carries real weight. It informs decisions and strengthens negotiations.

Case Study 2: The Surprised Florida Couple

A couple in Tampa found what they thought was the perfect starter home—$295,000, recently renovated, quiet street. They ran a quick online search and saw no major red flags.

Then they checked FEMA flood maps.

The property sat in an **X flood zone** (low risk), which seemed fine. But when they dug into historical NOAA storm surge data, they discovered something the listing didn't mention: the neighborhood flooded during Hurricane Ian, even though it was technically "low risk."

They requested the seller's insurance claims history. Sure enough: **$18,000 in flood damage** two years earlier.

They walked away immediately.

Two months later, they found a comparable home one mile inland—same price range, similar layout—but with zero flood claims and genuinely low NOAA storm surge exposure. Insurance cost them **$400 less per year**, and they sleep better knowing they actually understand their risk profile.

"Federal data doesn't just save money—it saves years of regret."

The Bottom Line

Here's what you now know that most homebuyers never learn:

The federal government already collected the most comprehensive property risk data in America. They mapped flood zones. They tracked earthquakes. They identified environmental hazards. They analyzed climate trends. They documented crime rates. They surveyed soil conditions. And they made all of it free and publicly accessible.

Most buyers never use it.

You're not "most buyers" anymore.

The seven federal databases—FEMA, USGS, EPA, NOAA, USDA, FBI, and Census—provide authoritative property intelligence that informs every major decision you'll make. The data already exists. The smart move is actually using it.

CHAPTER RECAP

□ **Federal databases are free, authoritative, and publicly accessible**—but most buyers never check them.

□ **Sellers, realtors, and inspectors aren't required to provide comprehensive risk analysis**—that responsibility falls on you.

□ **Seven agencies track the data that matters most:** FEMA (floods), USGS (earthquakes/landslides), EPA (environmental hazards), NOAA (climate/weather), USDA (soil), FBI (crime), and Census (demographics).

□ **Red flags include:** high flood insurance costs, Superfund site proximity, increasing wildfire risk, poor soil drainage, and rising crime rates.

□ **Two approaches work:** manually checking all seven databases (takes 45-60 minutes per property) or using an aggregation service like Home Data Reports (takes 5 minutes, costs less than dinner out).

□ **Real buyers have used federal data to negotiate tens of thousands in price reductions**—not because they hired experts, but because they simply looked up what the government already documented.

□ **Next step:** Now that you know where the data comes from, it's time to understand what it actually means. In Part 2, we'll walk through each major risk category—starting with the most common and costly of all: flood exposure.

Now that you know **where** the data comes from, it's time to understand what it actually means. In **Part 2**, we'll walk through each of the seven major risk categories—what they are, how they affect your property, how to identify them quickly, and what steps to take if you find them.

Let's start with the most common and costly risk of all: flood exposure...

Chapter Resources

Feel free to skip ahead if you'd like to continue reading.

----

trying to make sense of flood zone codes, seismic probabilities, or Superfund distances.

Test our risk calculator on your target properties—it takes 30 seconds and gives you an instant snapshot of flood, fire, earthquake, environmental, and climate risk scores. Download our free Chrome extension to check properties in real-time while you browse listings online.

And here's the thing: if this information helped you, it'll help the people you care about. Share **HomeDataReports.com** with friends, family, and your real estate team. If you're a professional (realtor, lender, insurance agent), explore our partner program—you can offer these reports to clients and earn referral income while providing massive value.

Want to go deeper? Check out our video masterclass and digital toolkit for step-by-step training on using federal data like a pro.

Chapter 4

Flood & Water Risks

Sarah and Mike thought they'd done everything right.

They stretched to buy a **$415,000 starter home on the Gulf Coast**. The inspection was clean. The roof was solid, no obvious water damage. Their lender cleared them. They closed, moved in, and framed the "Welcome Home" photo on the mantle.

Two months later, they called an insurance agent to set up their homeowner's policy.

The agent pulled up their address, paused, and said: "You know you're in a FEMA flood zone, right? You're required to carry separate flood insurance."

The quote came back at **$3,800 per year just for flood insurance**. They had budgeted **$1,500 total** for all insurance. That's **$2,300 more every year** than planned—about **$69,000 over a 30-year mortgage**.

Sarah and Mike felt betrayed. Their realtor never mentioned flood costs. The seller "didn't think it was a big deal." Walking away wasn't an option; they were already locked in.

So they tightened the budget everywhere else. Fewer dinners out. Delayed vacations. Less savings. And one more worry: *Will this be harder to sell later?*

> *Flood risk lives in the cracks between everyone's job. You can close on a house, sign a mountain of paperwork, and never once see the word "flood" in a way that feels urgent or expensive.*

Most buyers don't *ignore* flood risk—they're just never really shown it.

Disclosure Gaps

Only about half of U.S. states have strong flood disclosure laws. States like Louisiana and Texas require sellers to disclose flood zones and past events. But many others have weak rules or **no flood disclosure requirement at all**. A seller can legally say nothing—even if the home has flooded multiple times.

Realtors aren't always trained to run FEMA map checks. Title companies focus on ownership and liens, not climate risk. Many sellers genuinely don't know their exact flood zone.

Result: you can close on a house and never hear about flood risk until the insurance bill arrives.

> ◻ **RED FLAG #1:** Seller says "It's never flooded" but can't produce proof of flood insurance history or FEMA zone documentation. Past flooding isn't always disclosed—especially if it happened before current ownership.

The "It's Never Flooded" Fallacy

You ask the seller, "Has it ever flooded?" They say no. That might be true for their five years of ownership. But what about the previous 20 years?

Here's the hard truth: **14.6 million U.S. properties face substantial flood risk**—nearly 70% more than the 8.7 million properties on FEMA's official maps. FEMA maps are often outdated, sometimes by decades. A home built in 1985 on "safe" land might now sit in a newly designated flood zone.

Climate projections show sea levels rising 10-12 inches by 2050 in many coastal areas. Insurance companies are adjusting rates accordingly—which is why premiums in high-risk zones have jumped from $2,000 to $5,000+ annually.

> *A home that hasn't flooded in the past doesn't mean it won't flood in the future. Maps change. Rainfall patterns change. Development changes.*

Understanding Flood Risk: Zones, Elevation, and Insurance

Understanding flood risk starts with knowing three things: **FEMA zones**, **Base Flood Elevation (BFE)**, and **insurance pricing**.

FEMA Flood Zones Explained

FEMA divides properties into zones:

Zone X (Minimal Risk): Low flood risk. Insurance optional, typically $400-$700 annually.

Zone A/AE (High Risk): 1% annual flood chance. Insurance **mandatory with mortgage**, typically $2,000-$5,000+ annually.

Zone V/VE (Coastal High Risk): High risk with wave action. Highest premiums, often $5,000-$10,000+ annually.

□ **STEP 1:** Go to FEMA's Flood Map Service Center (msc.fema.gov) and enter the property address. Note the exact zone designation.

Base Flood Elevation (BFE) Matters

Even within high-risk zones, **elevation makes a massive difference**. BFE is the level floodwaters are expected to reach during a 100-year flood. If a home sits **above BFE**, insurance costs drop significantly. If it sits **below BFE**, costs skyrocket.

A home in Zone AE sitting 2 feet above BFE might pay $1,800/year for flood insurance. The same zone with the home 1 foot *below* BFE? That premium could jump to $4,500/year.

□ **STEP 2:** Request an Elevation Certificate from the seller (if available) or order one through a licensed surveyor ($400-$800). This document shows the home's elevation relative to BFE.

Why Insurance Costs Vary So Much

FEMA's **Risk Rating 2.0** system (launched in 2021) uses property-specific factors to price flood insurance: distance to water, elevation above BFE, foundation type, flood history, and rebuilding costs.

Two homes on the same street can have wildly different premiums. One might pay $1,200/year, the other $4,000/year—based on minor elevation differences or foundation types.

Understanding your specific flood risk—not just the zone—lets you negotiate price, budget accurately, and avoid financial surprises after closing.

Warning Signs of Hidden Flood Risk

□ **RED FLAG #2:** The home has a sump pump, French drains, or significant grading work. These are often signs of past water intrusion—even if the seller doesn't mention flooding.

□ **RED FLAG #3:** Fresh paint on lower walls, new flooring, or recent basement renovations without explanation. These could indicate undisclosed flood repairs.

□ **RED FLAG #4:** The home sits in a "Moderate Risk" Zone X, but development upstream has changed drainage patterns. Moderate-risk zones are seeing more frequent flooding due to increased rainfall and urbanization.

□ **STEP 3:** During your home inspection, specifically ask the inspector to check for signs of past water damage: water stains, mold, warped floors, or rust on appliances.

Your Action Plan: What To Do Before You Buy

□ **STEP 4:** Get flood insurance quotes BEFORE making an offer. Call 2-3 insurance agents with the property address and zone. Ask for quotes based on different elevation scenarios.

□ **STEP 5:** Check the property's flood claim history through Home Data Reports or request a CLUE (Comprehensive Loss Underwriting Exchange) report. This shows prior insurance claims, including flood damage.

□ **STEP 6:** If the home is in a high-risk zone, calculate the true monthly cost including flood insurance. Add this to your mortgage payment to see if it still fits your budget.

Real Example: Jacksonville, Florida

A buyer found a home listed at $380,000 in Zone AE. Before making an offer:

1. Checked FEMA maps (confirmed Zone AE)
2. Ordered elevation certificate ($600)
3. Got insurance quotes ($3,200/year—6 inches below BFE)
4. Calculated total: $2,890/month vs. $2,350 budgeted

They walked away. No offer, no wasted fees, no emotional attachment. Two weeks later, they found a comparable home outside the flood zone for $375,000 with $800/year insurance.

Two minutes of research can save you tens of thousands of dollars, years of stress, and a lifetime of financial clarity.

Does This Risk Matter To You?

This book isn't about scaring you away from flood-prone homes. Some buyers are perfectly comfortable with flood risk if they budget for it. The key is that **you choose knowingly, not accidentally**.

Flood risk might be acceptable if:

- You've budgeted for higher insurance comfortably
- The property sits above BFE
- You plan to invest in mitigation
- The location checks every other box

Flood risk might be a dealbreaker if:

- Insurance costs push payments out of reach
- You prefer predictability
- Climate projections show worsening risk
- Comparable homes exist without exposure

There's no right answer—only an informed one.

A flood zone isn't a dealbreaker if you know about it and budget for it. The problem is discovering it after closing.

The key takeaway from this chapter is simple: **Flood risk is one of the most common and costly property risks—but also one of the easiest to check. FEMA data is free and public. Use it.**

Success Story

A couple shopping in Tampa Bay found their perfect home—a **$445,000 property** in a top school zone. Before submitting an offer, they ran a comprehensive property intelligence report.

The home was in an **AE flood zone** with **$4,200/year** estimated insurance. A comparable home two streets over (outside the flood zone) had **$1,200/year** insurance. That's a **$3,000 annual difference**—or **$90,000 over 30 years**.

They didn't panic. They used the information to negotiate.

They submitted an offer **$40,000 below asking**, backed with clear flood insurance math. The seller countered with a **$30,000 reduction**, which they accepted. Between the price reduction and their awareness of long-term insurance costs, they got a fair deal with zero surprises.

They didn't avoid flood risk. They bought with knowledge—and negotiated from strength. That's the difference.

□ **What You Learned:**

- Half of U.S. states have weak or no flood disclosure laws
- 14.6 million properties face flood risk—70% more than FEMA maps show
- FEMA zones (X, A/AE, V/VE) determine mandatory insurance requirements

- Elevation above BFE drastically impacts insurance costs ($1,800 vs. $4,500+/year)
- Check FEMA maps, order elevation certificates, and get insurance quotes BEFORE making an offer
- A flood zone isn't a dealbreaker if you budget for it and negotiate accordingly
- Two minutes of research can save $69,000+ over 30 years

Flood risk is just one piece of the puzzle. Next up: hurricane and severe weather risk. If you're buying in a storm-prone area (and climate change is expanding that definition), here's what you need to know...

Chapter 5

Hurricane Risk — The $24,000 Surprise

Jennifer and Tom did everything "right."

They stretched to buy a $485,000 home on the North Carolina coast. Great schools, fresh roof, quiet cul-de-sac. Their agent called it a "solid house in a solid neighborhood." The inspection came back clean. Insurance was bundled into their mortgage payment, so they didn't think much about the details.

Their first hurricane season felt more like a weather channel event than a personal threat.

A Category 3 storm spun up offshore and made landfall about 50 miles away. They never saw the eye. Just long bands of wind and rain, a night of howling gusts, and a morning of shingles scattered across the yard.

When an adjuster confirmed roughly $35,000 in roof and exterior damage, they were shaken—but hopeful. "That's why we have insurance," Tom said.

Then the letter arrived.

Because the damage was tied to a named storm, their regular $2,500 deductible didn't apply. Their policy carried a **5% named storm deductible**—5% of the **insured value** of the home, not 5% of the damage.

Five percent of $485,000 is $24,250.

That was their out-of-pocket bill **before** insurance would pay a single dollar.

"They didn't buy in a hurricane zone by mistake. They bought into hurricane risk without understanding how the money works."

No one had ever walked them through this. Not the lender who rolled the policy into their payment. Not the agent who said "you're fully covered." Not the seller, who never mentioned previous hurricane claims. The storm never even hit them directly—landfall was an hour's drive away—but the National Weather Service warning was enough to trigger the higher deductible.

They couldn't write a $24,000 check. They financed the repairs, added a second monthly payment, and started putting aside an extra $200 a month into what they now call their "hurricane fund." Vacations got delayed. Renovation plans disappeared.

Why Buyers Miss Hurricane Risk

Hurricane risk feels like background weather, not a line item on the spreadsheet. Most buyers are juggling inspections, appraisals, and moving logistics. That's how real financial danger slips through.

The Disclosure Problem

There is **no federal requirement** that sellers disclose hurricane or flood history. Florida—the epicenter of hurricane risk—does **not** require sellers to disclose prior flooding at all.

> □ **RED FLAG #1:** Florida does not require sellers to disclose previous flood damage. You could be buying a home with a hidden hurricane claim history.

Named storm deductibles (2–5% of your home's insured value) sit deep in policy documents most buyers never read. Lenders just need proof of coverage to close. Millions of buyers relocating from non-coastal states are used to a simple $1,000–$2,500 deductible—not a system where a hurricane warning can trigger a $15,000–$25,000 bill.

The Named Storm Deductible Trap

On a typical policy, your standard deductible might be $1,500. But in hurricane country, there's a second line: **named storm deductible: 2–5% of the insured value**.

On a $400,000 house, that's **$8,000–$20,000 out-of-pocket per storm** before insurance pays anything.

> **Jamie Tracey, Port Salerno, Florida (October 2024)**
>
> A 71-year-old retiree took a hit from Hurricane Milton tornado warnings. Her home suffered $30,000 in damage. She filed a claim expecting reasonable costs.
>
> Instead: **$14,000 hurricane deductible** (5% of her building coverage). She'd believed the 5% applied to damages only, not home value.
>
> "I was going to have to mortgage my house out just to pay my deductible." The $14,000 represented 47% of total damage—devastating for a fixed-income homeowner.

The Financial Cascade

Miss hurricane risk up front, and you face a stack of problems:

- Coastal premiums reach **$8,000–$12,000 per year** (vs. $2,300 national average)
- Named storm deductibles create **$10,000–$25,000 exposure** every season
- Major insurers like State Farm and Allstate have **exited Florida entirely**
- Nearly **1 in 5 homeowners are uninsured** in some high-risk counties
- Homes sit on market longer as buyers back out during insurance due diligence

> □ **RED FLAG #2:** Major insurers like State Farm and Allstate have stopped writing new policies in Florida. If the pros won't take the risk, what does that tell you?

Hurricane risk is significant and expensive—but predictable. When you understand how insurance works and what deductibles look like, you can budget **before** you buy instead of being surprised after closing.

How Hurricane Risk Actually Works

Understanding hurricane risk means understanding the system **around** storms: insurance, deductibles, wind forces, and flooding.

The Three Hurricane Zones

Coastal High Risk (0–1 mile): Storm surge floods streets before rain begins. Category 3+ winds peel roofs. Insurance: **$3,000–$8,000/year**. Deductibles: **5–10%** of home value ($25,000–$50,000 on a $500,000 home).

Coastal Moderate (1–10 miles): Outside surge zones but wind still damages roofs and siding. Insurance: **$2,000–$4,000/year**. Deductibles: **2–5%** ($8,000–$20,000 on a $400,000 home).

Inland (10+ miles): Flooding from rain bands, tornadoes, days-long power outages. Insurance: **$1,500–$3,000/year**. Deductibles: Still apply if NWS issues hurricane warnings for your county—even 50+ miles from landfall.

"You don't need a direct hit to face a $24,000 deductible. You just need a hurricane warning."

Wind Mitigation Saves Money

Impact windows, roof reinforcement, and garage doors can **cut premiums by 10–45%**. Florida offers grants up to $10,000 for upgrades. But full mitigation costs **$5,000–$25,000**.

Warning Signs & Your Action Checklist

□ **RED FLAG #3:** The seller drops the price $20,000+ with no explanation after a recent hurricane season.

□ **RED FLAG #4:** Your insurance quote is 3x expected, or agents say "we don't write new policies there." When the market screams, listen.

"If major insurance carriers won't write new policies in the area, that's the market screaming at you."

This book isn't about scaring you away from homes. It's about giving you the information to make decisions that are right for YOU. A flood zone might be a dealbreaker for one family but perfectly acceptable to another who's budgeted for it. What matters is that you **KNOW before you buy**—not discover it after closing.

□ **ACTION STEP 1:** Get 3 insurance quotes **before** making an offer. Ask: "What is my named storm deductible in dollars?" Get it in writing.

□ **ACTION STEP 2:** Run a property intelligence report from **HomeDataReports.com** before your offer. You'll get hurricane exposure, storm history, and flood zones in one report.

□ **ACTION STEP 3:** Budget $200–$500/month for a "hurricane fund" to cover your deductible. If you can't afford this plus your mortgage, you can't afford the house.

□ **ACTION STEP 4:** Check FEMA flood maps and ask the county about "substantial damage" designations. This can kill deals days before closing.

□ **ACTION STEP 5:** Negotiate seller credits for impact windows or roof reinforcement using insurance quotes as leverage.

"If you can't budget $200–$500/month for a hurricane fund, you can't afford a coastal home."

Smart Buying on the Florida Coast

The biggest lesson from this chapter is simple: **hurricane risk is significant and expensive—but predictable.** When you understand how insurance works, what deductibles look like, and how storm patterns behave, you can plan for the cost **before** you buy instead of being surprised after closing. Coastal living can be wonderful. It just requires informed budgeting, not guesswork.

Aaron and Melissa: Tampa Coastal Buyers (2024)

Aaron and Melissa, a couple relocating from Colorado to Tampa, fell in love with a $520,000 home just two miles from the beach—exactly the lifestyle they wanted. Before making an offer, they ran a comprehensive property intelligence report. It revealed that the home sat in a high hurricane exposure zone and that the neighborhood had been hit by a Category 3 storm in 2017.

Instead of panicking, they dug deeper. Insurance quotes came back at **$4,200 per year**, plus a **5% named storm deductible**—roughly **$26,000** for their home's insured value. A comparable inland property had premiums closer to **$1,800 a year** with no special deductible.

They didn't walk away. They simply adjusted their offer. Aaron and Melissa submitted a bid **$45,000 below asking**, citing insurance cost differences and storm exposure. The seller countered with a **$35,000 reduction**, which they accepted. They also secured a **$15,000 seller credit** for impact window installation.

Their total benefit: **$50,000 in savings and credits**.

Today, they budget about **$350 per month** for insurance and their hurricane fund. They maintain a **$30,000 emergency reserve** for their deductible and accept that evacuation may be necessary once or twice a decade. They love the coastal lifestyle—and they planned for it.

The lesson: They chose a hurricane zone **with clarity and preparation**. That's smart buying.

"Aaron and Melissa negotiated $50,000 in savings because they understood the insurance math before making an offer."

Chapter 5 Key Takeaways

□ Named storm deductibles are 2–5% of your home's **insured value**—potentially $10,000–$50,000 out-of-pocket per storm.

□ Major insurers have exited Florida's coastal markets, leaving 1 in 5 homeowners uninsured in some counties.

□ Florida does **not** require sellers to disclose prior flood damage—you could buy a home with hidden claims.

□ Wind mitigation upgrades cut premiums by 10–45% but cost $5,000–$25,000. Negotiate before closing.

□ You face the deductible with just a hurricane warning for your county—the storm can be 50+ miles away.

□ Get 3 insurance quotes **before** making offers and use them to negotiate seller credits.

Hurricane risk affects millions across the Gulf and Atlantic coasts. But what about the West? Earthquake risk is different—sudden, unpredictable, and often uninsured. If you're buying west of the Rockies, the ground beneath your feet might be the biggest risk factor of all.

Chapter Resources

Feel free to skip ahead if you'd like to continue reading.

Don't Let Hurricane Insurance Blindside You.

You just read about the $24,000 surprise. Now imagine knowing your exact hurricane risk—and insurance costs—before you ever make an offer.

HomeDataReports.com provides detailed hurricane risk analysis including storm surge zones, wind speed projections, historical hurricane paths, and projected climate impacts. We show you what Category 3, 4, and 5 storms could mean for your property—and your wallet.

Sign up for free and get your first Essential Report at no cost. Test our risk calculator to see hurricane scores for any coastal or inland property. Download our free Chrome extension to evaluate hurricane risk while browsing listings in Florida, Texas, Louisiana, the Carolinas, or anywhere hurricanes matter.

For insurance agents: Our partner program is designed for you. Provide clients with comprehensive hurricane risk reports before they bind coverage—it positions you as a trusted advisor, not just a policy seller. Realtors and lenders, the same applies: showing buyers their hurricane risk upfront prevents deals from falling apart at the insurance stage.

This chapter could save someone you know tens of thousands of dollars. Share **HomeDataReports.com** with friends on the coast or anyone considering a move to hurricane-prone areas.

Want the full training? Our video masterclass walks through hurricane risk analysis step-by-step, with real examples and negotiation strategies.

Chapter 6

Earthquake & Seismic Risks: The National Blind Spot

Jennifer and Tom closed on a $585,000 California home built in 1978. Fresh paint, clean inspection. "A solid house," their agent said.

Eight months later, a 5.4-magnitude earthquake hit. From the street, their home looked fine. Inside: cracked drywall, broken doors, shattered dishes.

They called their insurance company. The response stopped them cold:

"You don't have earthquake coverage—that's a separate policy."

The quote: $3,200 per year with a 15% deductible. On their home, that meant **$87,750 out-of-pocket** before insurance would help. Then they learned their 1970s home had never been retrofitted—estimated cost $25,000–$40,000.

Now every aftershock felt like a financial decision. Their neighbors admitted they had no earthquake insurance either. Too expensive.

That's when Jennifer and Tom realized how many people are gambling with their biggest asset without knowing it.

Most buyers treat earthquakes like background noise—something that happens "out there," not something that should shape their offer price or insurance strategy.

The California Myth—Busted

When most people hear "earthquake," they picture California. Wrong.

The latest U.S. Geological Survey shows **nearly 75% of the United States is at risk of damaging earthquakes.** Not California alone—**37 states have experienced magnitude 5.0+ earthquakes** in the last 200 years.

This includes the Pacific Northwest (Cascadia Subduction Zone—capable of magnitude 8.0–9.2 quakes). The New Madrid zone in Missouri, Tennessee, Arkansas, Kentucky—with a **25–40% chance** of magnitude 6.0+ in 50 years. Charleston, South Carolina. Alaska, Hawaii, Nevada, Utah.

"I'm not in California" does NOT mean "I'm not at risk."

□ **RED FLAG #1:** Home built before 1980 in ANY state west of the Rockies—or in Missouri, Tennessee, Arkansas, Kentucky, South Carolina. These homes often predate modern seismic codes and may lack critical structural reinforcements.

The Insurance Gap Nobody Talks About

Most buyers assume: "If my lender approved the mortgage, I'm covered." Wrong.

Standard homeowners policies **exclude** earthquake damage. Earthquake insurance is a separate policy. Lenders rarely require it—even in high-risk zones.

Result? Only **10–13% of California homeowners** have earthquake insurance. In the 2014 Napa Valley earthquake, **less than 6% had coverage**—total losses reached billions.

Deductibles aren't $1,000 or $2,500. They're **10–20% of your dwelling limit.**

On a $500,000 home with 15% deductible, you pay **$75,000 out of pocket** before coverage begins—plus $2,000–$4,000 annual premiums.

□ **ACTION STEP 1:** Before making an offer, check the USGS National Seismic Hazard Map for your property's address. If it shows moderate-to-high risk, factor seismic evaluation into your due diligence.

How Construction Type Determines Your Risk

Most Vulnerable: Unreinforced Masonry (URM)

Pre-1960 brick or stone with **no internal steel.** Strong vertically, weak sideways—exactly how earthquakes move structures. Seattle has **over 1,000 URM buildings, 80% unretrofitted.** Retrofit costs: $30,000–$75,000+.

High Vulnerability: Soft-Story Buildings

Open parking/garages below, living space above. Past earthquakes: ground floors collapsed, upper floors pancaked onto garages. Retrofit: $50,000–$150,000+ per building.

Moderate: Pre-1980 Wood-Frame Homes

Not bolted to foundations. Home slides off, cripple walls collapse. Retrofits: $3,000–$15,000.

Lower Risk: Post-2000 Construction

Built to updated seismic codes with foundation bolting, shear walls, moment frames. Dramatically safer.

> □ **RED FLAG #2:** Large, unbraced brick chimney on pre-1980 home. Chimneys are among the most common sources of catastrophic damage during earthquakes.

The Hidden Retrofit Costs

Pre-1980 homes weren't built to today's seismic standards. Buyers learn about costs after they're committed.

Foundation bolting: $3,000–$8,000 | Cripple wall bracing: $2,000–$7,000 | Shear walls: $5,000–$15,000 | Soft-story retrofits: $50,000–$150,000 | Chimney work: $2,000–$10,000

These upgrades reduce collapse risk and lower insurance premiums 10–25%. Some cities mandate retrofits—most don't. Unless you ask, "Has this home been retrofitted?" the answer rarely appears.

Disclosure Gaps

Most states don't require earthquake disclosures. California has the strongest requirements, but documentation is often incomplete.

Reality: Sellers may not know if homes were retrofitted. Standard inspectors aren't structural engineers. Permit records can be incomplete.

Major earthquakes are separated by decades. People discount the risk. But when shaking arrives, repair bills reach tens of thousands to $100,000+. One event can erase a lifetime of equity.

□ **ACTION STEP 2:** For pre-1980 homes, hire a structural engineer (not just inspector) to evaluate seismic vulnerabilities. Cost: $400–$800. Can save $50,000+ in surprise bills.

□ **RED FLAG #3:** Soft-story construction—garage/parking below living space. This configuration has repeatedly failed. Ask: "Has this building been retrofitted?"

In the 2014 Napa Valley earthquake, less than 6% of homeowners had earthquake insurance—even though total losses reached into the billions.

The Resale Value Factor

Seismic risk affects resale. Informed buyers now ask: Is the home retrofitted? Is insurance available and affordable?

Retrofitted homes sell for **$20,000–$50,000 more** than unretrofitted homes. Buyers see them as safer and easier to insure. As cities adopt retrofit ordinances, older unretrofitted properties may become harder to finance or sell.

□ **ACTION STEP 3:** Get earthquake insurance quotes BEFORE closing. Factor the annual premium and deductible into total ownership costs. Unmanageable cost = critical information for offer negotiation.

□ **ACTION STEP 4:** Check if the city has mandatory retrofit ordinances. If your building falls under these rules but hasn't been retrofitted, you could inherit a legal deadline and a six-figure bill.

Earthquake risk is NOT just California—42 states have moderate-to-high risk. The danger isn't the shaking—it's the insurance gaps, retrofit costs, and disclosure blind spots that catch buyers after closing.

Does This Risk Matter To You?

This isn't about scaring you away. It's about making informed decisions.

A seismically vulnerable home might be a dealbreaker for one family but acceptable to another who's budgeted for retrofits and insurance. What matters: you KNOW before buying—not after closing.

Truth: **Old homes can be made earthquake-safe.** Retrofits work. Insurance exists. Risk becomes manageable when you plan upfront—factor retrofit costs into your offer, secure insurance before closing, build an emergency fund for the deductible.

Couples who regret their purchase never knew to ask. Couples who thrive entered with open eyes and a plan.

□ **ACTION STEP 5:** If buying in a seismic zone, create a 3-year plan: **Year 1**—Complete critical retrofits using seller credit or savings. **Year 2**—Secure earthquake insurance and understand your deductible. **Year 3**—Build an emergency fund equal to your deductible amount.

Retrofitted homes can sell for $20,000–$50,000 more than similar unretrofitted homes because buyers see them as safer and easier to insure.

SUCCESS STORY: THE PORTLAND CRAFTSMAN

A couple searching in Portland, Oregon—inside the Cascadia Subduction Zone—fell in love with a $485,000 Craftsman built in 1924. Beautiful character, perfect neighborhood.

They ran a property risk report before making an offer. It showed **high seismic risk**. They hired a structural engineer who confirmed what many older Portland homes need: foundation bolting and cripple wall bracing. Retrofit cost: **$18,000.** Earthquake insurance quote: **$2,400/year** with **15% deductible—$72,750** out-of-pocket in a major event.

Instead of walking away, they made a plan.

They offered **$455,000—6.2% below asking**—using the retrofit estimate and insurance burden to justify their price. They provided the engineering report and insurance quote. Seller countered at **$465,000** with a **$15,000 retrofit credit.** They agreed.

They completed the seismic retrofit using the credit, secured earthquake insurance, and committed to building a $75,000 emergency fund over three years.

Net outcome: **$20,000 purchase savings + $15,000 retrofit credit = $35,000 total value.** Their home is now safer than most in the neighborhood, with documented retrofit boosting future resale value.

Lesson: They didn't fear seismic risk—they managed it with data, negotiation, and planning.

Chapter 6 Key Takeaways

□ Earthquake risk extends far beyond California—75% of the U.S. could experience damaging earthquakes, including the Pacific Northwest, New Madrid region, and Charleston, SC

□ Standard homeowners insurance EXCLUDES earthquake damage—it's always a separate policy with 10–20% deductibles (often $75,000+ out-of-pocket)

□ Only 10–13% of California homeowners have earthquake insurance; most discover they're uninsured after damage occurs

□ Pre-1980 homes often lack critical seismic reinforcements; retrofits cost $3,000–$15,000 for wood-frame homes, $30,000–$150,000 for masonry or soft-story buildings

□ Unreinforced masonry and soft-story buildings are the most dangerous—many cities now mandate retrofits, which could become the new owner's legal obligation

□ Hire a structural engineer (not just a home inspector) for pre-1980 homes in seismic zones—this $400–$800 evaluation can save $50,000+ in surprise costs

□ Retrofitted homes sell for $20,000–$50,000 more than unretrofitted homes and are easier to insure—this isn't just a safety investment, it's a resale value boost

----

Chapter Resources

Feel free to skip ahead if you'd like to continue reading.

Understand Your Earthquake Risk—Even Outside California.

Most people think earthquakes only matter in California. As you just learned, that's dangerously wrong. The New Madrid Seismic Zone, the Cascadia Subduction Zone, and dozens of other fault systems put millions of homes at risk—and most buyers have no idea.

At **HomeDataReports.com**, our reports include USGS seismic hazard data, fault line proximity, historical earthquake activity, and projected ground shaking probabilities. We show you exactly what seismic risk looks like for your property—whether you're in San Francisco, Seattle, Salt Lake City, Charleston, or Memphis.

Create your free account and download your first Essential Report at no cost. Run our risk calculator to see earthquake scores for any U.S. address. Grab our free Chrome extension to check seismic risk in real-time while browsing properties online.

For professionals: Earthquake risk is one of the most overlooked aspects of real estate transactions. Join our partner network and provide clients with seismic risk reports—it's a differentiator that builds trust and prevents costly surprises. Home inspectors, this is especially powerful as a complement to your foundation and structural assessments.

If you know someone buying in California, the Pacific Northwest, the Intermountain West, or even the Midwest, send them to **HomeDataReports.com** —Earthquake insurance can cost $800-$3,000+ annually—worth knowing before closing.

Chapter 7

Wildfire Risks

Sarah got the letter on a Tuesday.

"We regret to inform you that State Farm will not renew your homeowners insurance policy." No explanation. No warning. Just thirty days to find new coverage on their $485,000 mountain home in Boulder County, Colorado.

They'd owned the house for three years. Never filed a claim. Premium always paid on time. But their home sat in what planners call the **Wildland-Urban Interface**—the WUI—where neighborhoods meet forests.

Sarah called five insurers. Three said no immediately. Two quoted premiums triple what she'd been paying. The only affordable option was the state's high-risk pool at $9,200 per year.

Insurance companies don't wait for fires to happen. They exit high-risk markets years before disaster strikes.

The fire risk was always there. Sarah just didn't know it mattered until her coverage vanished.

When Insurance Companies Abandon Entire Counties

Over 46 million American homes now sit in the WUI. That's one-third of all U.S. housing. These aren't just rural cabins. They're suburban developments, mountain communities, and canyon neighborhoods where trees meet rooftops.

California alone lost seven major insurers between 2023 and 2025. State Farm stopped writing new policies. Allstate pulled out entirely. Farmers dramatically reduced coverage. The pattern repeated in Colorado, Oregon, and Washington.

Homeowners who bought these properties thinking they were safe discovered reality too late. Their insurance wasn't canceled after a fire. It was **canceled before one could start**.

☐ **RED FLAG #1:** Your insurance carrier's stability matters more than your premium cost. If major insurers are exiting your state or county, that's a market signal—not a coincidence.

The January 2025 Palisades Fire in California destroyed properties averaging $4 million in value. But the real story wasn't the fire itself. It was what happened after.

One Altadena homeowner received $1.1 million from State Farm against a $3.1 million reconstruction estimate. Another family's premium jumped from $1,200 to $9,750 annually after rebuilding with fire-resistant materials. Home hardening didn't guarantee affordable insurance—it just kept them barely insurable.

This isn't about preventing fires. It's about **understanding the financial ecosystem** before you buy.

Paradise, California - Five Years After Camp Fire

After the 2018 Camp Fire destroyed 13,000+ homes, one homeowner rebuilt carefully. Metal roof. Stucco siding. Cleared defensible space. Everything by the book.

Her insurance premium: $1,200 annually in 2019. By 2024: $9,750. A 712% increase. Another couple saw Farmers Insurance jump from $2,800 to $9,550.

Home hardening worked to prevent fire damage. But it didn't prevent insurance from becoming unaffordable. The risk shifted from fire destruction to **financial suffocation**.

How Fires Actually Destroy Homes (And How To Stop Them)

Most people think wildfires work like Hollywood shows them. Walls of flames consuming everything in their path. That happens. But it's not the main threat.

The real killer is **ember attacks**.

☐ **ACTION STEP 1:** Check your home's vents, eaves, and deck gaps. Embers enter through quarter-inch openings and ignite homes from the inside.

Wind-blown embers can travel over a mile ahead of the main fire. They land on wood decks, lodge in roof valleys, slip through attic vents. A single ember finding dry vegetation or exposed wood can ignite a home while the fire front is still miles away.

This is why **defensible space** matters. It's not about creating a fireproof fortress. It's about eliminating fuel sources within 100 feet of your structure.

Zone 1 (0-5 feet from home): Remove all vegetation. Replace wood mulch with gravel. Move firewood storage away from walls.

Zone 2 (5-30 feet): Space trees 10 feet apart. Trim branches 6-10 feet from ground. Remove dead plants immediately.

Zone 3 (30-100 feet): Thin tree density. Create fuel breaks. Keep grass mowed below 4 inches.

A home hardened against embers can survive while the forest around it burns.
But an exposed deck or wood shake roof negates everything else.

Home hardening focuses on three critical areas: roof, vents, and decks.

Roofs: Class A fire-rated materials (composition, tile, metal). Wood shake roofs are uninsurable in most WUI areas now.

Vents: Ember-resistant mesh (1/8 inch maximum). Attic, crawl space, and foundation vents all need protection.

Decks: Composite or heavy timber construction. Wood decking acts as a massive fuel source touching your home.

□ **ACTION STEP 2:** Request your property's Wildfire Risk Assessment score BEFORE making an offer. Don't rely on real estate agents to disclose this voluntarily.

What Most Buyers Miss During Property Tours

Some warning signs appear obvious. Dense forest within 50 feet. Cedar shake roof. Wood siding. But others hide in plain sight.

□ **RED FLAG #2:** Check the road access. Many mountain communities have single-lane roads with no turnouts. Evacuation routes clog fast. If you can't leave quickly, reconsider the location.

Look at neighboring properties. If nearby homes have cleared defensible space but the house you're viewing hasn't, that tells you something about the current owner's priorities. You'll inherit their deferred maintenance.

Check utility line clearance. Trees within 10 feet of power lines create ignition risk. California utilities now face liability for fire-starting equipment, but that doesn't help you if your home burns.

Slope matters more than most buyers realize. Fire travels uphill 2-4 times faster than on flat ground. A home on a steep slope below dense vegetation faces exponentially higher risk.

Review your homeowners association rules. Some HOAs restrict defensible space clearing, tree removal, and fire-resistant upgrades. If the HOA prevents you from implementing fire mitigation, walk away.

□ **RED FLAG #3:** Recent insurance non-renewals in the neighborhood signal market retreat. Ask your agent directly: "What percentage of properties in this ZIP code have lost coverage in the past year?"

Get Insurance Quotes Before You Offer (Not After)

This step saves deals or kills them early—before you're emotionally invested.

□ **ACTION STEP 3:** Contact three insurance carriers BEFORE submitting your offer. Get written quotes with the property address. Don't accept "we'll figure it out at closing."

Most buyers wait until escrow to shop insurance. That's backwards. The time to discover you're uninsurable is during your inspection period—when you can still walk away.

Request these specific answers from insurers:

- Will you write a new policy on this property?
- What's the annual premium for replacement cost coverage?
- What wildfire mitigation would reduce that premium by at least 15%?
- Has your company stopped writing new policies in this county?

If two of three carriers refuse coverage, reconsider the purchase. If all three quote premiums exceeding 3% of purchase price annually, factor that into your offer.

The gap between "insurable" and "affordably insurable" determines whether your home becomes an investment or an albatross.

Get hardening cost estimates before closing. Hire a FireWise specialist to assess the property. Typical costs:

- Composite deck replacement: $8,000-$15,000
- Ember-resistant vents: $2,000-$4,000
- Class A roof replacement: $12,000-$25,000
- Defensible space creation: $5,000-$10,000 initial + $2,000-$4,000 annual maintenance

□ **ACTION STEP 4:** Request a mitigation credit from the seller if hardening work hasn't been completed. Documented costs justify price reductions of $15,000-$30,000 on WUI properties.

Does This Risk Matter To You?

This book isn't about scaring you away from mountain living. It's about knowing what you're committing to before you sign.

Some families thrive in WUI locations. They value forest access, wildlife, and privacy more than fire certainty. They budget for high insurance, commit to annual defensible space maintenance, and accept evacuation risk.

That's a legitimate choice—if you make it with open eyes.

WUI living requires active participation. You can't buy a forest home and ignore fire risk the way you ignore tornado risk in Kansas. The forest demands maintenance.

But if you're expecting low maintenance, stable insurance costs, and easy resale, WUI properties deliver none of those. The commitment isn't one-time. It's annual. Defensible space maintenance. Insurance shopping. Equipment upgrades. Evacuation planning.

Ask yourself honestly: Will you clear brush every spring? Will you replace that wood deck even though it's expensive? Will you trim trees annually even when it looks fine?

If the answer is "probably not," choose a different location. The forest won't compromise with neglect.

When The Numbers Actually Work

Daniel and Rebecca fell in love with a Boulder County property near where the Marshall Fire had recently destroyed an entire neighborhood. The seller wanted $695,000. They knew better than to make an offer first.

They hired a FireWise specialist who provided detailed mitigation estimates. Replace wood deck with composite: $12,000. Install ember-resistant vents: $3,000. Create defensible space: $8,000 initial plus $4,000 annually. Clear oak brush and thin trees: $6,000.

Total hardening cost: $29,000 upfront plus ongoing maintenance.

□ **ACTION STEP 5:** Use documented mitigation costs as negotiation leverage. Hard numbers from licensed contractors justify lower offers on high-risk properties.

Insurance quotes came back at $5,400 per year—more than double comparable properties in lower-risk areas. Armed with real numbers, they offered $625,000. The seller countered at $645,000 with a $15,000 mitigation credit.

They accepted. Completed all recommended hardening immediately. Invested an additional $14,000 of their own funds. Secured a $4,000 annual defensible space maintenance contract.

Daniel & Rebecca's Five-Year Outcome

Purchase price: $645,000 (after $15,000 seller credit) Total mitigation investment: $29,000 (first year) Annual maintenance: $4,000 Insurance: $5,400/year (with 10% FireWise discount)

Their home is now FireWise certified. Insurance remained stable through two carrier exits in neighboring ZIPs. When another family two streets over lost State Farm coverage, Daniel and Rebecca's certified status kept their policy active.

They sleep well because they didn't ignore the risk. They addressed it systematically—with numbers, not hope.

Insurance companies reward documented fire mitigation. But they're leaving high-risk markets regardless. Get written quotes early—before your heart overrules your spreadsheet.

Wildfire risk is manageable if you commit to ongoing work. But insurance market collapse is unpredictable. Check availability before you buy. Don't discover you're uninsurable after closing.

Chapter 7 Key Takeaways

□ Over 46 million U.S. homes sit in Wildland-Urban Interface zones where fire risk is expanding rapidly

□ Insurance companies are exiting high-risk markets before fires occur—not after

□ Ember attacks destroy more homes than direct flame contact—home hardening focuses on vents, roofs, and decks

□ Get insurance quotes from three carriers BEFORE submitting your offer—unaffordability kills deals late

□ Defensible space requires $5,000-$10,000 initial investment plus $2,000-$4,000 annual maintenance

□ Use documented mitigation costs as negotiation leverage—FireWise assessments justify price reductions

□ WUI living demands active commitment—if you won't maintain defensible space annually, choose a different location

----

Chapter Resources

Feel free to skip ahead if you'd like to continue reading.

See Your Wildfire Risk Before the Smoke Clears.

Wildfire zones are expanding. Insurance companies are pulling out of high-risk areas. Premiums are tripling. And most buyers don't realize they're in a danger zone until after they close.

HomeDataReports.com deliver comprehensive wildfire risk analysis including fire hazard severity zones, historical wildfire data, vegetation density, climate projections, and insurance market trends. We show you not just if a property is at risk, but what that means for your safety and your budget.

Open your free account today and get your first Essential Report completely free. Use our proprietary risk calculator to evaluate wildfire scores for mountain, foothill, or rural properties anywhere in the U.S. Download our Chrome extension to check wildfire risk instantly while browsing listings in California, Colorado, Oregon, Washington, Arizona, or other fire-prone states.

For insurance agents, realtors, and lenders: Wildfire risk is becoming a dealbreaker in more transactions every year. Our partner referral program lets you offer wildfire risk reports to clients as part of your standard service—it prevents last-minute insurance surprises that kill deals and damage relationships. Join at **HomeDataReports.com**.

Share this chapter with anyone considering mountain, foothill, or rural properties. Wildfire risk is no longer just a "California problem"—it's a national issue that requires data-driven decisions.

Our video masterclass includes a full module on wildfire risk assessment and mitigation strategies—check it out at **HomeDataReports.com** today.

Chapter 8

Environmental Hazards

The Invisible Threats That Show Up in Federal Databases

When the Kids Started Coughing

The Martinez family thought they'd found their dream home.

Four bedrooms, great schools, and a price that seemed almost too good to be true—$420,000 for a property that checked every box on their list. Their real estate agent called it a "steal." Comparable homes in nearby areas were listing for $475,000 to $490,000.

They moved in excited. Six months later, their excitement turned to concern.

Both kids developed persistent respiratory issues. Doctor visits became routine. Inhalers appeared in backpacks. The pediatrician asked questions about their home environment—mold, air quality, nearby industrial sites.

That's when they pulled a comprehensive property report.

> *Environmental contamination doesn't announce itself with visible damage. It hides in soil, water, and air—documented in free federal databases most buyers never check.*

The data revealed their "bargain" home sat less than one mile from an EPA Superfund site contaminated with industrial solvents. Just over a mile away, a Toxic Release Inventory facility released airborne emissions regularly. Health studies showed elevated cancer rates within this proximity zone.

Their below-market price wasn't a steal. It was a warning they'd missed.

Disclosure Laws Have Gaps You Can Drive a Truck Through

Federal law requires sellers to disclose "known" environmental hazards. That single word—known—creates massive loopholes.

Sellers aren't required to search EPA databases. They're not obligated to test for radon or lead paint unless they already know it exists. If they've never checked, they can legally claim ignorance.

This means roughly 27% of homes may have dangerous radon levels. About 29% contain lead-based paint. Thousands sit near Superfund sites or TRI facilities. Yet disclosure forms often arrive blank.

□ **RED FLAG #1:** Seller checks "no knowledge" on environmental disclosures. This doesn't mean safe—it means they never looked.

Here's what makes environmental risks particularly dangerous: they're invisible, long-term threats that standard home inspections don't catch. Your inspector checks the roof, foundation, and electrical systems. They don't test soil contamination or measure radon gas.

Meanwhile, the EPA maintains free public databases documenting contamination sites, toxic releases, and hazardous waste locations nationwide. Most buyers never access them.

□ **ACTION STEP 1:** Check EPA databases BEFORE making an offer, not after closing.

The cost of missing these risks? Buyers discover mercury contamination forcing evacuations. Families find PFAS in their well water. Homeowners learn their property sits on former landfill sites releasing methane gas. Insurance rarely covers environmental remediation, leaving buyers with six-figure cleanup bills.

How Environmental Hazards Actually Work

Environmental contamination falls into four main categories, each with distinct risks and data sources.

Category 1: Superfund Sites & Contaminated Land

The EPA's National Priorities List tracks over 1,300 severely contaminated locations across America. These Superfund sites contain heavy metals, industrial chemicals, and hazardous waste requiring long-term cleanup. Properties within one mile face measurable health risks and property value impacts.

Homes near Superfund sites sell for thousands less than comparable properties just miles away. The discount reflects real risk, not negotiating leverage.

Category 2: Toxic Release Inventory (TRI) Facilities

The EPA requires industrial facilities to report chemical releases annually. These TRI sites release substances into air, water, and land. Living near one means potential exposure to airborne toxins, groundwater contamination, and soil pollution.

Category 3: Radon & Lead Paint

Radon is a radioactive gas that seeps from underground granite and rock formations. You can't see it, smell it, or taste it. It's the second leading cause of lung cancer in America. Testing costs $150 to $300. Mitigation runs $800 to $2,500.

Lead paint remains in millions of older homes. It causes permanent neurological damage in children. Testing costs $300 to $500. Remediation ranges from $8,000 to $15,000.

□ **RED FLAG #2:** Home built before 1978 with no recent lead inspection. Lead paint was legal until that year.

Category 4: Underground Storage Tanks & Industrial History

Former gas stations, dry cleaners, and manufacturing sites often leave underground contamination. Leaking storage tanks release petroleum and chemicals into soil and groundwater. These sites require Phase I Environmental Site Assessments costing $1,900 to $3,500.

□ **ACTION STEP 2:** Research the property's historical use. Gas stations, dry cleaners, and industrial sites leave lasting contamination.

Here's how to check each risk:

EPA Superfund Map: Search by address for proximity to National Priorities List sites. Free at EPA.gov.

TRI Facility Database: Identifies industrial sites releasing toxic chemicals. Shows release volumes and chemical types. Free at EPA.gov.

Radon Zone Maps: EPA publishes county-level radon risk maps showing high-risk areas. Zone 1 indicates highest risk.

Lead Paint Risk: Any home built before 1978 requires testing if no recent inspection exists.

The EPA makes environmental data free and public. Your job is actually using it before you sign a purchase agreement.

Warning Signs of Environmental Risk

Watch for these indicators during your property search:

Property-Specific Flags:

Unusually low price compared to similar homes further away from industrial areas. Seller reluctance to provide environmental testing results. Property listed as "sold as-is" with minimal disclosures. Strange odors, discolored soil, or dead vegetation in the yard.

□ **RED FLAG #3:** Property priced $30,000+ below comparable homes nearby without clear explanation. Environmental risk often explains the discount.

Location-Based Flags:

Homes within 1-2 miles of industrial facilities, chemical plants, or manufacturing sites. Properties near former gas stations or dry cleaners. Areas with known groundwater contamination. Neighborhoods with historical industrial use.

□ **ACTION STEP 3:** Use Google Maps satellite view to identify industrial facilities near the property.

Testing and Disclosure Flags:

Seller checks "no knowledge" on environmental disclosure forms. No radon test results for homes in Zone 1 areas. No lead inspection for pre-1978 construction. Missing Phase I Environmental Assessment for commercial conversions.

Environmental hazards are documented, not hidden. The information exists in free federal databases. Most buyers simply don't look.

Check EPA Databases Before Making Your Offer

Follow this sequence for every property you consider:

Step 1: Search EPA Superfund Sites (5 minutes)

Visit the EPA Superfund website. Enter the property address. Check for National Priorities List sites within 3 miles. Note contamination types and cleanup status.

□ **ACTION STEP 4:** Search EPA Superfund database for the property address at EPA.gov/superfund.

Step 2: Check TRI Facility Database (5 minutes)

Access the EPA Toxics Release Inventory website. Enter the property ZIP code. Identify facilities releasing chemicals within 2 miles. Review released substance types and volumes.

Step 3: Verify Radon Risk Zone (2 minutes)

Check the EPA Radon Zone Map for the property county. Zone 1 indicates high risk requiring testing. Zone 2 suggests moderate risk. Zone 3 represents low risk.

Radon testing takes 48 hours and costs $200. Lung cancer treatment costs hundreds of thousands. The math isn't complicated.

Step 4: Research Property History (10 minutes)

Use Google Earth historical imagery to view past land use. Search county records for business licenses at that address. Check for former gas stations, industrial sites, or dry cleaners.

Step 5: Order Professional Testing If Needed

Radon test: $150-$300 for 48-hour test. Lead inspection: $300-$500 for certified inspector. Phase I Environmental Assessment: $1,900-$3,500 for commercial conversions or suspected contamination.

□ **ACTION STEP 5:** Add environmental testing contingencies to your purchase agreement. Make the offer conditional on acceptable results.

Step 6: Evaluate Results Before Closing

Superfund site within 1 mile: Consider walking away. TRI facility within 1 mile: Research emissions data and health studies. Radon above 4 pCi/L: Negotiate mitigation before closing. Lead paint confirmed: Get remediation quotes before finalizing.

□ **RED FLAG #4:** Seller refuses environmental testing contingencies. This suggests they already know something's wrong.

Does This Risk Matter to You?

Environmental hazards affect families differently based on health priorities and long-term plans.

Some buyers accept radon risks because mitigation systems work effectively. Others walk away from any contamination near their children. Both decisions are valid when made with complete information.

Consider these questions:

Do you have young children who are more vulnerable to lead paint and airborne toxins? Are you planning to stay long-term, increasing cumulative exposure? Can you afford remediation costs if testing reveals problems? Does your health insurance cover environmental illness treatment?

CASE STUDY: Choosing Safety Over Price

The Martinez family discovered their $420,000 home sat 0.8 miles from a Superfund site and 1.2 miles from a TRI facility. Comparable homes 3+ miles away sold for $475,000-$490,000. Their "bargain" reflected a $55,000-$70,000 contamination discount.

They walked away and purchased a similar home for $465,000—located 4 miles from documented hazards. They paid $45,000 more but gained no contamination risk, no health concerns, full property value, better resale prospects, and peace of mind for their children's health.

The data helps you decide what's right for YOUR family. A home near industrial sites might work for an investor planning to flip in two years. That same property could be wrong for a family raising kids for the next 15 years.

This book isn't about scaring you away from homes. It's about giving you information to make decisions that are right for YOU.

What matters is knowing before you buy, not discovering after closing.

Making the Right Call

The Martinez family made the harder choice. They paid more upfront but protected what mattered most—their children's health and their investment's value.

Three years later, their decision proved correct. The contaminated property they'd walked away from struggled to sell. Multiple buyers backed out after pulling environmental reports. When it finally sold, the price dropped another $35,000.

Meanwhile, their home appreciated normally. Their kids' respiratory issues disappeared. Their property value remained strong.

They paid $45,000 more. They gained something priceless: safety and stability.

That's what environmental due diligence delivers. Not fear. Not paranoia. Just accurate information helping you make the right decision for your family.

Some risks you can manage. Environmental contamination affecting your children's health isn't one of them.

The EPA maintains these databases for a reason. Use them. Check every property. Test when needed. Walk away if the data says run.

Your family's health isn't negotiable.

Chapter 8 Key Takeaways

□ Environmental hazards are documented in free EPA databases, but disclosure laws let sellers claim ignorance.

□ Four main categories: Superfund sites, TRI facilities, radon/lead paint, and underground contamination.

□ Properties near Superfund sites (within 1 mile) face measurable health risks and property value impacts.

□ Radon affects 27% of US homes; lead paint exists in 29% of housing units, mostly pre-1978 construction.

□ EPA databases (Superfund map, TRI tracker, radon zones) are free and searchable by address.

□ Environmental testing costs $150-$3,500 depending on scope—far less than discovering problems after closing.

□ Some families accept certain risks; others walk away entirely. Both decisions work when based on complete information.

Chapter 9

Climate Change Impacts

In 2018, Josh and Melissa bought their Phoenix dream home for $495,000. Three bedrooms, a pool, mountain views, and fifteen minutes to work. Friends congratulated them for getting in before prices really took off.

By 2024, the dream was melting.

Summer temperatures hit record highs forty-three days straight. Their AC ran nonstop, racking up $450 monthly bills. Insurance premiums jumped from $1,800 to $3,200 annually. Neighbors started selling at losses.

The house hadn't changed. The climate had.

Your mortgage runs until 2055. The climate you're buying into today won't be the climate you're living in by 2045.

The Thirty-Year Disconnect

Here's the disconnect: You're making a thirty-year decision based on today's weather.

Most buyers think short-term. "The summers are hot, but we'll manage." "Flood insurance costs a bit more, no big deal." They're assessing 2025 conditions for a property they'll own until 2055.

Climate scientists think differently. They measure decades, not seasons. And their data shows massive shifts coming in the next thirty years—exactly the lifespan of your mortgage.

This isn't about polar bears. It's about property values.

Research from First Street Foundation projects U.S. home values will drop $1.47 trillion by 2055, with 26% of neighborhoods entering what they call "climate abandonment" zones. These aren't disaster areas. They're places where rising costs and declining livability make homeownership financially unsustainable.

□ **RED FLAG #1:** If insurance companies are pulling out of your target market, that's a massive warning sign. They have billions at stake and analyze thirty-year risk models professionally.

How Climate Destroys Property Value

Climate change impacts property values through four mechanisms:

Insurance Market Collapse

Insurance companies operate on math. When the math says "we can't charge enough premium to cover the risk," they leave.

And they're leaving fast.

Florida homeowners now pay nearly $10,000 annually for coverage—highest in the nation. California's FAIR Plan (last-resort insurer) is receiving 1,000 new applications per weekday from homeowners abandoned by private insurers.

Seven of California's twelve top insurers have paused or restricted new business in the state. That's not a temporary adjustment. That's permanent retreat.

When a property becomes uninsurable, it becomes unmortgageable. No insurance means no financing. No financing means no buyers.

Paradise, California, saw the pattern play out after the 2018 Camp Fire. Insurance premiums jumped 37%. Population dropped 69%. Property values fell 42%.

Five years later, homeowners are still paying $10,000+ annually or going uninsured.

That's the reality of climate-vulnerable markets. Properties don't just lose value because of disasters. They lose value because the cost of protecting them becomes unbearable.

Temperature and Livability Changes

U.S. coastlines will see 10-12 inches of sea level rise by 2050—matching the entire previous century. Damaging floods that occurred once every 100 years will happen ten times more frequently.

Heat waves in Western states will increase four to five fold. Texas heat waves that lasted one week in the 1980s will last nearly two weeks by the 2050s.

This isn't theoretical. It's physics. The emissions are already in the atmosphere.

> Climate change operates on 30-year cycles. Your mortgage term matches that timeframe exactly. You're not buying weather conditions—you're buying climate trajectory.

Infrastructure Degradation

Extreme heat buckles roads. Aging water systems fail during floods. Electrical grids collapse during heat waves—exactly when you need AC most.

Baltimore's climate planning identified cascading failures across transportation, stormwater, water systems, and waste management. These failures directly reduce property values and increase maintenance costs.

Population Migration

When costs exceed tolerance, people leave. First Street's research shows climate migration is already underway, with population flowing from high-risk areas to climate "havens" in the Great Lakes, parts of the Midwest, and Pacific Northwest.

This creates a feedback loop: outmigration reduces demand, which lowers property values, which triggers more outmigration.

Property ownership in the 21st century increasingly depends on geographic luck—your location relative to climate risk.

The Warning Signs

> □ **RED FLAG #2:** Seven of California's twelve top insurers have paused new business in the state. That's not a short-term adjustment—that's permanent retreat.

> □ **RED FLAG #3:** If your target property is in a neighborhood where insurance premiums have doubled in five years, project what they'll cost in twenty-five years.

□ **RED FLAG #4:** Western states facing water restrictions are limiting new construction. If a region can't support growth, property values won't appreciate long-term.

Watch for:

- FAIR Plan enrollment spikes (last-resort insurance signal)
- Multiple consecutive years of extreme weather events
- Municipal infrastructure failures during disasters
- State emergency declarations becoming routine
- Net population outflow from previously desirable areas

□ **ACTION STEP 1:** Check First Street Foundation's Risk Factor tool for any property you're considering—it provides 30-year climate projections.

What You Should Do

Step 1: Assess Long-Term Climate Trajectory

Don't buy based on today's weather. Research projected conditions for 2045-2055.

Use NOAA's Climate Explorer for temperature and precipitation projections. Use NASA's sea level rise calculator for coastal properties. These are free federal tools with peer-reviewed data.

□ **ACTION STEP 2:** Run a 30-year insurance cost projection—if premiums double every decade, what's your total cost of ownership?

Step 2: Check Insurance Market Stability

Call multiple insurers before making an offer. Get actual quotes, not estimates. Ask about:

- Premium trends over the past five years
- Company's regional withdrawal plans
- FAIR Plan enrollment numbers in the area

If you can only get FAIR Plan coverage, that's a massive red flag.

□ **ACTION STEP 3:** Calculate total climate-adjusted cost of ownership—purchase price + insurance increases + utility cost increases over 30 years.

Step 3: Factor Climate into Your Budget

A $400,000 house in a climate-vulnerable area might cost you:

- $400,000 purchase price
- $300,000 in insurance premiums over 30 years (at increasing rates)
- $150,000 in additional cooling costs
- $50,000 in climate adaptation upgrades

That's $900,000 total—more than double the sticker price.

□ **ACTION STEP 4:** Compare properties in stable vs. vulnerable climates using 30-year total cost analysis, not just purchase price.

Step 4: Consider Climate-Resilient Regions

If long-term value matters more than current location, consider:

- Great Lakes region (water security, mild temperature increases)
- Pacific Northwest interior areas (stable climate, lower disaster risk)
- Parts of the Midwest and Mountain West with water access

These regions are seeing climate migration inflows, which supports long-term property appreciation.

Insurance markets are smarter than individual buyers. They're pricing 30-year risk right now. Follow their lead.

Does This Risk Matter To You?

Climate risk doesn't matter equally to everyone.

If you're planning to stay 5-7 years: Current insurance costs matter more than 2050 projections. You can often ride out short-term market conditions.

If you're buying a forever home: Climate trajectory is critical. You'll personally experience 2045-2055 conditions, and you need to plan accordingly.

If you're in your 30s-40s: Your mortgage term extends to 2055. You'll live through the full climate transition that scientists are projecting.

If you're near retirement: Your time horizon is shorter, but resale value still matters. Climate-vulnerable properties will be harder to sell as awareness grows.

CASE STUDY: PHOENIX TO ANN ARBOR

Josh and Melissa ran the 30-year numbers on their Phoenix home. Projected outcomes by 2050:

- Cooling costs: \$800-\$1,200/month (currently \$450)
- Insurance: 20% annual increases
- Property values: projected decline of 20-30%

They sold in 2024 and bought a \$545,000 home in Ann Arbor, Michigan. Their 30-year outlook:

- Stable freshwater supply
- Mild temperature increases
- Stable insurance market
- Strong economy (university anchor)
- Projected value appreciation

They paid \$50,000 more upfront but cut their 30-year ownership costs by an estimated \$400,000. That's strategic thinking.

The Payoff: Financial Security Based on Reality

Think in decades, not seasons, and you'll make better decisions than 95% of buyers.

The housing market is slowly catching up to climate reality. Buyers who position ahead of the curve—by choosing climate-resilient locations or demanding steep discounts in vulnerable areas—will protect their wealth over the next thirty years.

Josh and Melissa's move wasn't about fear. It was about math.

They accepted that their mortgage term runs to 2055, and they needed to buy accordingly. Today, they sleep well knowing their property won't become a stranded asset when the insurance market finally prices climate risk accurately.

That's the payoff: **financial security based on reality, not hope.**

Chapter 9 Key Takeaways

- ◻ Climate change operates on 30-year cycles—exactly matching your mortgage term
  - ◻ Insurance market retreat is the first and strongest warning signal
  - ◻ Project 2045-2055 conditions, not 2025 conditions
  - ◻ Calculate total cost of ownership including insurance and utility increases
  - ◻ Climate-vulnerable areas may see 20-40% property value declines by 2055
  - ◻ Climate-resilient regions are seeing migration inflows and value appreciation
  - ◻ Use federal tools (NOAA, NASA, First Street) for data-driven decisions

----

Chapter Resources

Feel free to skip ahead if you'd like to continue reading.

Plan for the Next 30 Years, Not Just Today.

You're not buying a home for 2025—you're buying it for 2030, 2040, 2050. Climate projections matter because they affect property values, insurance costs, and long-term livability.

HomeDataReports.com include climate change impact analysis based on NOAA sea-level rise projections, temperature trends, precipitation changes, extreme weather probabilities, and long-term risk modeling. We show you how your property's risk profile may evolve over the next 10, 20, and 30 years—so you can make decisions based on the future, not just the present.

Sign up for free and get your first Essential Report at no cost. Use our risk calculator to evaluate climate vulnerability for any U.S. property. Download our Chrome extension to check long-term climate projections while browsing listings.

For financial advisors, lenders, and realtors: Climate risk is becoming a factor in property valuations and mortgage underwriting. Our partner program allows you to offer climate impact reports as part of your advisory services—it positions you as forward-thinking and helps clients make smarter long-term investment decisions.

Share this chapter with friends considering coastal properties, river valleys, or areas with extreme heat projections. Climate data is predictive, not reactive—use it to your advantage.

Want deeper training on climate risk analysis? Check out our video masterclass and digital toolkit at **HomeDataReports.com**.

Chapter 10

Demographic & Crime Data

Mark and Alicia thought they'd done everything right.

They bought a $365,000 three-bedroom in a quiet suburb outside a major city. Tree-lined streets. Fresh paint. New roof. The listing photos showed kids riding bikes and dogs being walked at sunset. During their daytime showings, everything felt calm—mowed lawns, tidy driveways, neighbors waving as they drove by. They even did multiple walk-throughs at different times of day, just like the blogs suggested.

Six months after moving in, the picture changed.

Mark's car was broken into twice in their own driveway. Packages disappeared from the front porch often enough that they started shipping everything to Alicia's office. One night, police lights flashed down the block—someone had broken into their neighbor's home while the family was out to dinner.

"We never felt truly safe. Every noise at night made us jump. Every package delivery felt like a risk."

Mark started researching crime data—something he wished he'd done before buying. The FBI's Crime Data Explorer showed property crime rates in their ZIP code were 40% higher than the county average. Break-ins had increased 22% over the past three years. Police response times averaged 18 minutes for non-emergency calls.

The data had been publicly available the entire time.

Within two years, Mark and Alicia sold at a $15,000 loss and moved to a neighborhood where they'd done the research first. The stress, the lost money, and the constant anxiety—all preventable with an hour of research before they made an offer.

Why Buyers Skip the Research That Matters Most

Most homebuyers skip neighborhood safety research entirely. Not because the data doesn't exist—it's free and public—but because they don't know where to look or fear appearing discriminatory.

Let me be direct: **Researching crime trends is legal, responsible, and smart. Discriminating based on demographics is illegal, unethical, and wrong.**

The Fair Housing Act prohibits discrimination based on race, religion, national origin, familial status, disability, or sex. You cannot and should not use demographic data to exclude neighborhoods. That's not what this chapter teaches.

What you CAN do:

- Research objective crime statistics and trends
- Analyze police resources and response times
- Review economic indicators showing stability or decline
- Visit neighborhoods at different times of day
- Talk to current residents about their experiences

> □ **RED FLAG #1:** If your agent discourages you from researching crime data or makes demographic-based comments about neighborhoods, that's a Fair Housing Act violation. Report it and find a new agent.

Here's why buyers avoid this research:

Fear of Appearing Prejudiced

Many buyers worry that asking about neighborhood safety will make them look discriminatory. So they avoid the topic entirely—even though researching safety is both legal and prudent.

Confusion About What's Legal to Research

Buyers don't know the difference between researching crime trends (legal) and using demographics to make decisions (illegal). The uncertainty keeps them from researching at all.

Overwhelming Amount of Data

Crime data exists across federal, state, county, and city databases. Census information spans dozens of categories. Without knowing which metrics matter, buyers give up before they start.

> You can research safety responsibly. Focus on crime TRENDS (improving or worsening?), not demographics. Use objective data: police budgets, response times, property values, and infrastructure investment.

Real Estate Agent Avoidance

Many agents avoid safety discussions entirely to stay compliant with Fair Housing laws. While their caution is understandable, it leaves buyers navigating this research alone.

The result? Buyers make $300,000+ decisions based on gut feel during a 20-minute showing instead of reviewing objective data that predicts their actual lived experience.

How to Research Neighborhood Safety Responsibly

Responsible safety research focuses on objective trends and resources—not demographics. Here's the framework.

Federal Crime Data: FBI's Crime Data Explorer

The FBI maintains the most comprehensive national crime database through its Uniform Crime Reporting (UCR) Program. The Crime Data Explorer provides crime statistics by city, county, and state.

What You Can Find:

- Violent crime rates (assault, robbery, homicide)
- Property crime rates (burglary, theft, auto theft)
- Year-over-year trends (improving or worsening?)
- Comparisons to state and national averages

How to Use It:

1. Visit the FBI Crime Data Explorer website
2. Enter the city or county for your target property
3. Review the past 5 years of data
4. Look for trends, not isolated incidents

"A single bad year doesn't define a neighborhood. Look for consistent trends

over 3-5 years."

What to Look For:

- **Declining crime:** Property crime dropped 15% over 3 years = positive trend
- **Rising crime:** Break-ins increased 25% over 2 years = red flag
- **Stable crime:** Rates unchanged for 5 years = predictable environment

☐ **ACTION STEP 1:** Check the FBI Crime Data Explorer for your target city/county. Download the past 5 years of property crime data and identify trends.

Local Police Resources

Crime statistics tell you what happened. Police resources tell you what happens when you call for help.

Key Metrics:

- **Response time:** How long until officers arrive for non-emergency calls?
- **Police budget:** Is funding increasing or decreasing?
- **Officers per capita:** Are there enough officers for the population?
- **Police presence:** Do you see regular patrols?

How to Research:

1. Visit the local police department website
2. Request response time data (often published in annual reports)
3. Review budget documents (available through city/county websites)
4. Drive through the neighborhood at different times—do you see patrol cars?

☐ **RED FLAG #2:** If the local police department's budget has been cut multiple years in a row while crime rates increased, that's a warning sign about future safety.

Economic Indicators: Stability vs. Decline

Neighborhoods with strong economic fundamentals tend to have lower crime rates and better-maintained infrastructure. Here's what to research:

Property Value Trends:

- Are home values increasing, stable, or declining?
- Use Zillow, Redfin, or your county assessor's data
- Compare 5-year trends to the broader county

Owner-Occupancy Rates:

- High percentage of owner-occupied homes = stability
- High percentage of rentals = higher turnover and less community cohesion
- Check U.S. Census Bureau's American Community Survey (ACS)

"Neighborhoods where people invest and stay tend to have lower crime and stronger schools."

Employment and Income Trends:

- Is median household income rising or falling?
- What's the unemployment rate compared to the county?
- Are businesses opening or closing?

☐ **ACTION STEP 2:** Check the U.S. Census Bureau's QuickFacts for your target ZIP code. Look at owner-occupancy rates, median income, and unemployment compared to county averages.

Infrastructure Investment

Cities invest in neighborhoods they expect to grow. Look for:

Recent Improvements:

- New schools, parks, or libraries
- Road repaving and streetlight upgrades
- New businesses opening (coffee shops, grocery stores)

Deferred Maintenance:

- Potholes, broken streetlights, overgrown medians
- Boarded-up buildings, vacant lots
- Lack of public services (trash pickup, snow removal)

> Infrastructure investment signals where the city expects growth. Disinvestment signals declining priority and often correlates with rising crime.

School Quality as a Proxy (Use Carefully)

School ratings from sites like GreatSchools often correlate with property values and neighborhood stability. However, these ratings are controversial because they can reinforce segregation and penalize schools serving disadvantaged students.

What to Consider:

- Ratings can reflect socioeconomic factors more than teaching quality
- Visit schools in person and talk to parents for real insights
- Don't use school ratings as the sole decision factor

> □ **RED FLAG #3:** GreatSchools ratings are heavily criticized for bias. If school quality matters to you, visit the school, review test score trends (not absolute scores), and talk to current parents.

Multiple Neighborhood Visits

No amount of data replaces physically experiencing a neighborhood at different times.

Visit At Least 3 Times:

1. **Weekday morning (7-9 AM):** See the school commute and work traffic
2. **Weekday evening (5-7 PM):** Observe after-work activity and street presence
3. **Weekend afternoon (12-3 PM):** Check for community activity and maintenance

What to Observe:

- Are people outside walking, playing, gardening?
- Do homes look maintained (fresh paint, mowed lawns)?
- Are streets well-lit at night?
- Do you see broken windows, graffiti, or abandoned cars?

□ **ACTION STEP 3:** Visit your target neighborhood at three different times: morning, evening, and weekend. Bring a notebook and write down observations about activity, maintenance, and how you feel.

Talk to Residents:

Knock on doors. Introduce yourself as a potential buyer. Ask:

- "How long have you lived here?"
- "What do you like most about the neighborhood?"
- "Is there anything you wish you'd known before moving in?"
- "Do you feel safe here?"

Most people are happy to share their experiences—and their answers will tell you more than any database.

"The best neighborhood research tool is a 5-minute conversation with someone who actually lives there."

Warning Signs You Cannot Ignore

These are objective indicators that a neighborhood may have higher safety risks:

□ **RED FLAG #4:** Crime rates have increased year-over-year for 3+ consecutive years

□ **RED FLAG #5:** Police response times exceed 15 minutes for non-emergency calls, and the police budget has been cut

□ **RED FLAG #6:** Property values are declining while the broader county's values are rising

□ **RED FLAG #7:** Over 60% of homes are rentals, indicating high turnover and low community stability

□ **RED FLAG #8:** Visible signs of disinvestment: broken streetlights, potholes, boarded-up buildings, overgrown vacant lots

□ **ACTION STEP 4:** Review the red flag checklist for your target neighborhood. If 3 or more apply, seriously reconsider the purchase or negotiate a lower price to reflect increased risk.

Your Step-by-Step Research Process

Here's how to research neighborhood safety responsibly:

Step 1: Research Crime Trends (1 hour)

- Visit FBI Crime Data Explorer

- Pull 5 years of property and violent crime data
- Compare your target area to county and state averages
- Identify trends (improving, stable, or worsening?)

Step 2: Review Police Resources (30 minutes)

- Check police department website for response times
- Review budget documents (available through city/county sites)
- Look for news articles about police funding changes

Step 3: Analyze Economic Indicators (30 minutes)

- Census Bureau QuickFacts: owner-occupancy, income, unemployment
- Zillow/Redfin: 5-year property value trends
- Drive through: Are businesses opening or closing?

Step 4: Visit the Neighborhood 3 Times (2-3 hours total)

- Morning, evening, and weekend
- Observe activity, maintenance, street conditions
- Take photos and notes

Step 5: Talk to Current Residents (30-60 minutes)

- Knock on 3-5 doors
- Ask about their experience, safety concerns, and neighborhood changes
- Listen for consistency across multiple residents

□ **ACTION STEP 5:** Block out 5 hours over two weeks to complete all five research steps before making an offer.

Step 6: Review Infrastructure Investment

- Check city planning websites for upcoming projects
- Look for new parks, schools, or public improvements

- Identify areas of deferred maintenance

Step 7: Compile Your Findings
Create a simple one-page summary:

- Crime trend: Improving, stable, or worsening?
- Police resources: Adequate, strained, or underfunded?
- Economic indicators: Growing, stable, or declining?
- Infrastructure: Invested or neglected?
- Resident feedback: Positive, mixed, or concerning?

Use this summary to decide if the neighborhood aligns with your safety priorities.

Does This Risk Matter to You?

Not everyone prioritizes the same level of neighborhood safety. Your tolerance depends on:

Your Family Situation:

- Families with young children often prioritize low crime and walkability
- Empty nesters may accept slightly higher property crime if walkability and culture are strong
- Single professionals may prioritize urban amenities over ultra-low crime rates

Your Budget:

- Safer neighborhoods typically cost more
- You may accept higher crime risk in exchange for more house or better location

Your Experience:

- Urban residents often have higher tolerance for property crime than suburban buyers
- First-time buyers may not know what level of crime is "normal"

"This book isn't about scaring you away from homes. It's about giving you the information to make decisions that are right for YOU."

Questions to Ask Yourself:

1. Would I feel comfortable walking outside at night?
2. Would I let my kids play unsupervised in the yard or on the street?
3. Can I afford a security system if needed?
4. Am I comfortable with visible police presence?
5. Do I value urban culture enough to accept higher property crime rates?

> A flood zone might be a dealbreaker for one family but perfectly acceptable to another who's budgeted for flood insurance. The same applies to crime. What matters is that you KNOW before you buy—not discover it after closing.

If crime trends are worsening and you have young children, this may be a dealbreaker. If crime is stable but slightly higher than average and you're getting a great deal, you may accept it with proper precautions (security system, well-lit yard, strong locks).

The data gives you the power to decide what trade-offs you're willing to make.

> ☐ **ACTION STEP 6:** Have an honest conversation with your household: What level of crime risk is acceptable to us? Write down your priorities before you start shopping.

When Data-Driven Research Pays Off

Brad and Emma learned from Mark and Alicia's mistake.

When they started house shopping, they committed to researching neighborhoods first—then looking at houses second. They used the same budget and criteria but added objective crime and economic analysis to their process.

They identified three comparable neighborhoods with similar home prices around $365,000.

Neighborhood A:

Crime had increased 18% over three years. Police budget cuts reduced patrol presence. Property values lagged county growth by 30%. Multiple residents mentioned package theft and car break-ins.

They passed immediately.

Neighborhood B:

Crime rates declined 12% over five years. Police funding increased modestly. Strong owner-occupancy (78%). Property values grew 6% per year, outperforming the city's 4% average. Infrastructure was well-maintained—new streetlights, repaved roads, and a renovated park. Residents they spoke with praised the tight-knit community.

This became a strong contender.

Brad and Emma's Smart Trade-Off:

They chose Neighborhood B, even though it meant buying a smaller home. The house was 200 square feet less than what they could afford in Neighborhood A. But the data showed declining crime, strong property values, and satisfied residents.

Three years later:

- Zero crime incidents
- Strong relationships with neighbors
- Home value increased to $395,000 (8.2% annual growth)
- Their children play outside safely every day
- Total peace of mind

The trade-off was worth it. They bought less house but gained the right neighborhood.

Neighborhood C:

Comparable safety metrics to Neighborhood B, but the economics were weaker. Property values had been flat for three years, and the high percentage of rental homes signaled transience. They passed again.

Their Decision:

They purchased in **Neighborhood B** for $365,000. The home was 200 square feet smaller than they could have bought in Neighborhood A, but the data told a clear story.

Three years later:

- Zero crime incidents
- Strong community relationships
- Home value increased to $395,000
- Children play outside safely

- Total peace of mind

They chose data over aesthetics—and it paid off.

"We bought less house but gained the right neighborhood. That's a trade-off we'd make again every single time."

Chapter 10 Key Takeaways

□ **Crime research is legal and responsible—profiling is not.** Focus on trends, not demographics.

□ **Use FBI Crime Data Explorer to analyze 5 years of crime trends.** Look for improving, stable, or worsening patterns.

□ **Review police resources:** Response times, budget trends, and patrol presence matter as much as crime statistics.

□ **Economic indicators predict safety:** Owner-occupancy rates, property value trends, and infrastructure investment signal neighborhood trajectory.

□ **Visit neighborhoods 3 times at different times of day.** Your observations will tell you more than any database.

□ **Talk to current residents.** Ask direct questions about safety, changes, and their lived experience.

□ **Red flags:** Rising crime + declining police budgets + falling property values + high rental rates = serious concern.

□ **Your safety tolerance is personal.** Define your priorities before house shopping, not during.

Chapter Resources

Feel free to skip ahead if you'd like to continue reading.

Understand the Neighborhood, Not Just the House.

Property values aren't just about square footage and granite countertops—they're about neighborhood trends, demographic shifts, and safety. And most buyers never look at the data.

At **HomeDataReports.com**, our reports include Census demographic data, crime statistics, school ratings, economic trends, population growth or decline, and neighborhood stability indicators. We show you not just what the neighborhood looks like today, but where it's heading.

Create your free account and download your first Essential Report free when you sign up. Run our risk calculator to see how any neighborhood scores across safety, demographics, and long-term stability. Download our Chrome extension to check neighborhood data in real-time while browsing listings—perfect for families evaluating school districts and safety.

For realtors: Neighborhood data is one of your biggest value-adds to clients. Our partner referral program lets you provide comprehensive neighborhood reports as part of your listing presentations or buyer consultations. It's a differentiator that builds trust and helps clients make confident decisions about location.

If you know someone relocating to a new city or state, send them to **HomeDataReports.com** — Understanding neighborhood trends before you buy is just as important as understanding the property itself.

Chapter 11

Pulling It All Together

You've learned about seven major property risk categories. But here's the reality: properties don't have just ONE risk. They have combinations. And when risks stack, they amplify each other.

Think about a coastal property in Florida that looks perfect on paper. Walkable to the beach. Palm trees out front. Sunset views. Listed at $575,000 in a nice neighborhood—perfectly "normal" for the area.

Underneath the photos, it has three overlapping risks:

First, it sits in a FEMA AE flood zone. Mandatory flood insurance, with maps already adjusting for rising seas.

Second, it's in a Category 3+ hurricane exposure zone. High winds, storm surge, and named-storm deductibles tied to the full insured value of the home—not the damage.

Third, sea level projections show one to two feet of rise by 2050. That means chronic "sunny day" flooding and more frequent storm impacts over your 30-year mortgage.

Now layer in the money: Flood insurance runs $2,500 annually. Hurricane insurance adds $4,200, with a five percent named-storm deductible—that's $28,750 out of pocket before insurance pays anything. Total annual insurance: $6,700. Over 30 years, that's more than $200,000 in insurance premiums alone.

> *When risks compound, they don't just increase your costs—they multiply your exposure.*

This isn't fear-mongering. This is math. And math doesn't care about sunset views.

Why Multiple Risks Hurt More Than You'd Expect

Most buyers assume risks add linearly. "Flood zone adds five percent risk. Hurricane adds another five percent. That's ten percent total."

Wrong.

When risks overlap, they interact. A property with just flood risk might see a three to five percent value discount. But combine flood plus hurricane plus sea level rise, and you're looking at 15 to 20 percent discounts—plus insurance becoming unavailable or prohibitively expensive.

Research from 2025 shows more than 2.4 million Florida properties face combined reconstruction costs of $667.5 billion at moderate or greater risk of storm surge damage.

In Miami, homes inside the 100-year flood zone experience value reductions of nine to 18 percent per square foot. Median flood insurance premiums nearly doubled under Risk Rating 2.0—jumping from $787 to $1,402 annually for a single-family home.

Homeowners in Miami now face the highest insurance burden among top U.S. metros, with premiums consuming 3.7 percent of market value annually. New Orleans is second at 3.6 percent.

> □ **RED FLAG #1:** When annual insurance costs exceed three percent of property value, lenders get nervous. Above five percent, many won't approve loans at all.

Real Examples: How Risk Stacking Plays Out

Tampa Bay: A buyer purchased a $575,000 property in 2022. The seller said insurance was "normal for the area." After closing, actual costs hit: flood insurance $2,500 annually, hurricane coverage $4,200, plus a $28,750 named-storm deductible.

By 2024, their insurance reached $10,200 annually after carrier exits forced them to more expensive options. Thirty-year projection: potentially $300,000+ in insurance premiums. They thought they bought a $575,000 home. The effective cost approaches $875,000.

Tampa Bay: The $300K Insurance Trap

Property purchased 2022: $575,000 Initial insurance estimate: $3,200/year

Actual costs after closing:

- Flood insurance: $2,500/year
- Hurricane/windstorm: $4,200/year
- Named-storm deductible: $28,750 per event

2024: Insurance hits $10,200/year (+219% from estimate)

30-year projection: $300,000+ Effective property cost: $875,000

Oakland Hills, California: Properties facing wildfire plus earthquake plus liquefaction now see annual insurance exceeding $15,000. Multiple carriers refuse to write policies. One homeowner's premium jumped from $8,200 in 2023 to $14,300 in 2025—with a $50,000 deductible.

The real cost of a property isn't the purchase price. It's the purchase price plus the lifetime cost of managing its risks.

Evaluating Risk Combinations

Not all combinations are equal. Some amplify dramatically. Others remain manageable with proper planning.

High-Risk Combinations (Avoid Unless Exceptional Circumstances):

Flood + Hurricane + Sea Level Rise creates compounding exposure. Each risk makes the others worse. Insurance becomes progressively unaffordable or unavailable within 10-15 years.

Wildfire + Earthquake can trigger simultaneously. Insurance companies won't adequately cover both. Self-insuring means absorbing six-figure losses.

Environmental Contamination + Flood Zone creates toxic exposure during flooding. Remediation costs multiply. Some properties become permanently unmarketable.

□ **RED FLAG #2:** Properties with three or more overlapping major risks often become uninsurable within 5-10 years. Today's affordable policy could be tomorrow's denial.

Moderate-Risk Combinations (Manageable with Planning):

Hurricane + Standard Flood Risk is common in coastal areas. Expensive but insurable if you budget correctly. Shop multiple carriers and lock in multi-year policies when available.

Lower-Risk Combinations (Often Acceptable Trade-offs):

Older Infrastructure + Stable Geology means aging systems are fixable. Plumbing, electrical, and HVAC updates are one-time investments that don't compound annually.

Radon + Standard Home Features requires a $1,500-$3,000 mitigation system. Once installed, it's done. Not a recurring cost.

The goal isn't finding a risk-free property. The goal is finding a property where risks are manageable, insurable, and predictable over your ownership timeline.

The Three-Property Comparison Method

Never evaluate a property in isolation. Human psychology tricks you. You fall in love with granite countertops while ignoring the flood zone.

Compare three properties side-by-side with full cost accounting.

Calculate True 30-Year Cost:

- Purchase price
- Plus: 30-year insurance projection
- Plus: Known mitigation costs
- Plus: Major system replacements

This gives you the "effective cost" of ownership.

Example:

Property A (Coastal): $575K purchase + $201K insurance + $45K systems = **$821K effective cost**

Property B (Inland): $525K purchase + $45K insurance + $40K systems = **$610K effective cost**

Property C (Canal): $540K purchase + $120K insurance + $90K systems/seawall = **$750K effective cost**

When you convert lifestyle choices into long-term dollar amounts, clarity appears.

Now the real questions: Is Property A's beach access worth $211,000 more than Property B over 30 years? That's $7,000 per year. For some buyers, absolutely. For others, no.

Is Property C's water view worth $140,000 more than Property B? You decide based on your actual lifestyle and budget.

□ **ACTION STEP 1:** Before viewing properties, define your three non-negotiables and your maximum acceptable 30-year insurance cost.

□ **ACTION STEP 2:** Create a spreadsheet with three columns. Fill in every cost for all three properties. Calculate 30-year totals.

Assessing Your Own Risk Tolerance

Risk tolerance isn't about bravery. It's about financial capacity plus psychological resilience.

Financial capacity: Can you absorb a $50,000 uninsured loss? Can you handle annual insurance doubling in five years?

Psychological resilience: Can you sleep at night in a flood zone? Will you stress every hurricane season?

Three clarifying questions:

What's your financial runway?

- Six months emergency fund = Choose minimal-risk properties
- 12+ months = Some manageable combinations acceptable
- 24+ months = Can absorb unexpected insurance spikes

What's your ownership timeline?

- 5-7 years = Risks matter less
- 10-15 years = Risks matter significantly
- 20-30 years = Risks matter tremendously

What's your backup plan?

- If insurance becomes unavailable, can you self-insure?
- If property values decline, can you afford to stay?
- If mitigation becomes required, can you fund it?

If you answered "no" to Question 3, you need low-risk properties. Period.

□ **ACTION STEP 3:** Write down your answers to all three questions. Share them with your partner. Agreement on risk tolerance prevents fights later.

Risk tolerance changes with your financial position, life stage, and circumstances. Reassess it before every home purchase.

Using Risk Knowledge for Negotiation

Most sellers don't fully understand their property's risk profile. Most buyers don't ask the right questions. You now have an information advantage.

Leverage Point: Insurance Reality Check

Get actual insurance quotes during your inspection period. When quotes come back at $6,000 annually versus the seller's claimed $2,500, you have concrete negotiation power.

Script: "Based on actual quotes from three carriers, the true cost of ownership is $3,500 higher annually than represented. That's $105,000 over 30 years. I'm asking for a $50,000 price reduction to offset this."

□ **ACTION STEP 4:** Include insurance quote contingency in your offer. Reserve the right to renegotiate if actual quotes exceed representations by 25% or more.

□ **RED FLAG #3:** If the seller refuses to provide current insurance documentation, that signals they know there's a problem. Require disclosure or walk.

The Pre-Offer Checklist

Before making any offer, run through this checklist. Three or more red flags? Reconsider.

Combined Risk Assessment:

- How many major risk categories? (0-2 = manageable, 3+ = caution)
- Are risks compounding or independent?
- Can I get insurance from multiple carriers?
- What's the 30-year insurance projection?

Financial Reality:

- Does the 30-year cost fit my budget?

- Can I absorb 50-100% insurance increases?
- Do I have reserves for mitigation?

Lifestyle Value:

- Does this property justify the risk premium?
- Have I compared at least two alternatives?
- Am I deciding based on data or emotion?

□ **ACTION STEP 5:** Print this checklist. Complete it BEFORE making offers. Keep it in your car during tours.

The best home purchase is one you can still afford and still want ten years from now when insurance has doubled and risks have compounded.

What Comes Next

You understand how risks interact and compound. You have a framework for comparing properties objectively. You know how to assess your risk tolerance honestly.

The next chapter walks you through the pre-offer checklist in detail—every data point to verify, every question to ask, every contingency to include.

Because pulling it all together isn't just about understanding risks. It's about using that understanding to make the smartest decision for YOUR situation, YOUR timeline, and YOUR financial future.

Chapter 11 Key Takeaways

□ Risks don't add—they compound. Three overlapping risks create 3-5X the exposure of single risks.

□ High-risk combinations often become uninsurable within 5-10 years.

□ The three-property comparison method eliminates emotional bias.

□ True property cost = purchase price + 30-year insurance + mitigation + systems.

□ Risk tolerance depends on financial capacity AND psychological resilience.

□ Information about actual insurance costs creates massive negotiation leverage.

□ Never make an offer without comparing at least three properties with full cost accounting.

Chapter Resources
Feel free to skip ahead if you'd like to continue reading.

See the Complete Picture—In One Report.

You've learned about flood zones, hurricanes, earthquakes, wildfires, environmental hazards, climate risks, and neighborhood data. Now imagine having all of that information—for any U.S. property—delivered in a single, easy-to-read report.

That's exactly what **HomeDataReports.com** do. We aggregate 10+ federal data sources into comprehensive property intelligence reports that show you the complete risk profile in minutes, not weeks.

Sign up for free and get your first Essential Report at no cost when you create your account. Test our proprietary risk calculator on multiple properties to compare options side-by-side. Download our Chrome extension and check properties instantly while browsing Zillow, Redfin, or Realtor.com—it's like having a property intelligence dashboard built into your browser.

This is where everything comes together. No more jumping between FEMA maps, EPA databases, USGS seismic zones, and NOAA climate projections. One address, one report, complete clarity.

For professionals: Our partner referral program is built for realtors, lenders, insurance agents, home inspectors, and contractors who want to offer clients a complete property intelligence solution. Join the network and start providing comprehensive risk reports as part of your service offering.

Share **HomeDataReports.com** with anyone shopping for a home. This is the tool you wish existed when you started your search—now it does.

Want the full training on how to use comprehensive reports in your property search and negotiation? Our video masterclass and digital toolkit walk you through the entire process step-by-step.

Chapter 12

Your Pre-Offer Checklist

Carlos thought he'd done everything right.

He toured the home twice. He ran an insurance quote. He skimmed the disclosure form. The neighborhood felt calm, the price seemed fair, and nothing obvious stood out. So he made an offer—quickly, because the market was moving fast.

Three weeks later, during the inspection period, he found what he'd missed.

The home sat 0.4 miles from a former industrial site that had been remediated but still carried monitoring requirements. The inspector found early signs of moisture around the slab foundation. And a deeper look at the county records showed the home had been inside a historical flood zone before maps were updated. None of these issues were catastrophic on their own—but together, they shaped the true long-term cost of the property.

When the dust settled, Carlos said something every buyer eventually realizes: "I thought I'd checked enough. I hadn't."

A simple checklist—used before he made the offer—would have caught everything early and saved days of stress, renegotiation, and uncertainty.

"I thought I'd checked enough. I hadn't." — A lesson every unprepared buyer learns the hard way.

This is the chapter that prevents that experience.

Most buyers do research in a scattered, emotional way. They look at a few listings, run a quick insurance estimate, ask the agent a couple of questions, and assume they have the full picture. But homebuying is too complex for "good enough." You've learned about seven major risk categories—flood, hurricane, wildfire, earthquake, environmental hazards, climate change, and neighborhood trends. Now you need a system to make sure you review all of them for every property you consider.

Because here's the truth: our brains skip steps. We remember the pretty kitchen, not the deductible. We note the updated roof, not the nearby Superfund site. We forget to check crime trends because the neighborhood "felt safe" during a 20-minute showing. Emotion kicks in, and important details fall through the cracks. That's human nature, not a personal flaw.

Checklists fix that.

Pilots use them. Surgeons use them. Engineers use them. Not because they lack skill, but because checklists ensure nothing critical gets overlooked when the stakes are high. The same principle applies to real estate. A pre-offer checklist protects you from avoidable mistakes and forces you to evaluate a home based on facts—not excitement, pressure, or assumptions.

Checklists turn chaotic, emotional decisions into calm, systematic evaluations.

And here's the encouraging part: this process isn't complicated. It takes two to three hours per property. But those hours can prevent $50,000 to $500,000 in long-term surprises. A checklist turns a chaotic, emotional decision into a calm, systematic evaluation. It gives you confidence in every offer you make, because you know you didn't miss anything important.

This book has never been about avoiding risk. It's about understanding risk—so you can decide what fits your budget, your priorities, and the lifestyle you want. The goal of a pre-offer checklist isn't perfection. It's clarity. It helps you ask the right questions, verify the right data, and make a decision that aligns with your risk tolerance, not someone else's.

Your Seven-Category Checklist

Here is a seven-category pre-offer checklist for every serious property. You're not chasing perfection—just making sure you see the full picture before you write an offer.

Flood & Water Risks

□ **ACTION STEP 1:** Look up the address on FEMA's Flood Map Service Center and note the flood zone.

□ **ACTION STEP 2:** Call two insurance agents and get flood quotes using this address and a rough price.

□ **ACTION STEP 3:** Search the address plus "flood" in local news or county records to see if it has flooded before.

□ **RED FLAG:** Property is in a Special Flood Hazard Area and quotes exceed what you can comfortably budget each year.

Hurricane & Wind Risks

For hurricane and wind risks, use your state's insurance or hurricane website to see if the address is in a named-storm or wind-borne debris zone. Ask three insurers for written quotes showing the wind or hurricane deductible in dollars. Check the listing or property appraiser site for roof age and material. If the hurricane deductible would drain most of your emergency fund, pause before offering.

Earthquake & Seismic Risks

□ **ACTION STEP 4:** Check USGS earthquake hazard maps to see if you're in a moderate or high shaking zone.

Note the home's year built and compare it to major seismic code updates. If you're in a high-risk zone and the home was built before updated codes, budget for a structural engineer's review before you close.

Wildfire Risks

Check wildfire risk by reviewing state fire hazard maps or tools like Cal Fire's severity zones. Look at the property's defensible space—how much clearance exists between structures and vegetation. Ask your insurance agent if the property requires wildfire mitigation before coverage is available.

□ **RED FLAG:** Property is in a high or very high fire hazard severity zone with dense vegetation and no clear defensible space.

Environmental Hazards

Environmental hazards don't announce themselves—you have to actively search for them.

Search the EPA's Superfund site database and review the Toxics Release Inventory for the ZIP code. Check state and county databases for known contamination, underground storage tanks, or remediation sites within one mile. Look at radon zone maps and ask if the home has been tested recently.

Climate Change Considerations

Climate change considerations include reviewing NOAA's sea level rise projections if the property is coastal, checking historical temperature and precipitation trends, and evaluating how insurance costs might shift over your ownership period. This isn't about predicting decades ahead—it's about understanding the direction of change.

Neighborhood Trends

□ **ACTION STEP 5:** Review neighborhood crime statistics using local police department data or third-party tools.

□ **ACTION STEP 6:** Check school ratings if relevant to your family's needs.

Review crime statistics, check school ratings if relevant, and look at recent sales data to see if property values are stable, rising, or declining. Drive through the neighborhood at different times of day to get a sense of activity patterns and maintenance standards.

The checklist doesn't guarantee a perfect home—it guarantees you understand the risks before you commit.

The Go/No-Go Framework

Once you've completed your checklist, you need a decision framework. Not every risk is equal, and not every property with risks should be rejected. This is where the Go/No-Go framework comes in—a simple way to turn data into action.

Green light properties have zero to one risk flags, insurance that fits your budget, and no significant concerns across the seven categories. These homes move forward with confidence.

Most homes you consider will live in the messy middle—where smart buyers pause, dig deeper, and then decide with both eyes open.

Yellow light properties have two to three risk flags—but the flags are manageable, insurance is available (even if elevated), and you have a clear mitigation plan. Yellow does not mean "bad." It means "more homework, then decide." For the right buyer with the right budget and risk tolerance, yellow light properties can become excellent deals.

□ **RED FLAG:** Four or more risk flags or one critical risk like major environmental contamination or uninsurable status.

Red light properties have four or more risk flags or one critical risk (like major environmental contamination or uninsurable status). Insurance is unavailable or far beyond your budget. Mitigation costs exceed what you can realistically cover. Most buyers should walk away. If you decide to proceed, your offer should reflect the true risk—often 20-40% below comparable sales—with seller-paid mitigation as a condition of closing.

A buyer discovered a home was in a high-risk flood zone, near an industrial site, with rapidly rising insurance costs and multiple past claims.

Their checklist lit up across flood, environmental, and insurance categories.

Instead of "hoping for the best," they treated it as a red light and moved on.

Months later, that same home relisted after another buyer's deal fell apart during the insurance process.

Their decision saved them from years of stress.

Remember: a red light does not mean the property is "bad" for everyone. An investor with a large cash reserve and short timeline might see opportunity where you see unacceptable risk. That is the point—this is about alignment with your finances and your peace of mind.

> The Go/No-Go framework turns data into decisions. Your risk tolerance + property characteristics = clear next steps.

Your Seven-Day Timeline

A clear timeline makes this entire process feel simple and manageable. You're not trying to analyze every detail in one sitting—you're spreading the work across a few days so you can move confidently without feeling rushed.

Day 1 (Initial Property Review — 30 minutes)

Your goal on day one is to answer one question: Is this property worth deeper research? Start with a quick FEMA flood zone check, a basic search of the address with terms like "flood," "fire," or "disaster," and a look at county property records. Finish with one insurance quote to confirm the property is insurable at a level you can afford. If any of these raise major concerns, you can move on before investing more time.

> ☐ **ACTION STEP 7:** Set aside one focused block of time to run the full seven-category checklist.

Day 2-3 (Deep Dive Research — 2-3 hours)

Once a property passes your initial screen, it's time to run the full seven-category checklist. This includes gathering multiple insurance quotes, checking environmental databases, reviewing wildfire and seismic maps, and pulling climate projections. Most of this research is online and free. By the end of this phase, you'll have the clearest picture most buyers ever get before making an offer.

Day 4-5 (Professional Consultations — varies)

These steps are only needed if your checklist revealed areas that deserve professional eyes. Examples include ordering an elevation certificate for homes in flood-prone areas, consulting a structural engineer if earthquake risks appear significant, or getting a fire mitigation assessment in wildfire regions. Not every property needs these, but when they do, this is where you get answers that matter.

Start with potential deal-breakers first. If insurance premiums come back far beyond your budget, there's no need to research six other categories.

Day 6-7 (Decision & Offer Prep)

Now you compile everything. Apply the Go/No-Go framework, calculate long-term costs, and determine whether the property aligns with your budget and risk tolerance. If it does, you're ready to prepare your offer strategy with confidence, knowing you're negotiating from a position of knowledge—not assumption.

Efficiency strategies: Start with potential deal-breakers first. Use a spreadsheet to track each property. Batch your insurance quote requests. Keep all screenshots and notes in one folder. The more organized you are, the faster each new property becomes.

If you're in a hot market: Speed and diligence can work together. Focus on the three categories most relevant to the property type or location, get those answers within 24-48 hours, then complete the remaining categories while your offer is being considered. Even partial research gives you a major advantage over buyers who rely solely on emotion or appearance.

One buyer followed a timeline like this when evaluating a charming $600,000 home.

Their checklist revealed recent but undisclosed foundation repair work and flooring replacement.

After confirming the details with the repair company, they realized these issues were significant enough to impact long-term value.

Instead of moving forward blindly, they used the findings to renegotiate, saving tens of thousands of dollars and preventing future stress.

This is the power of a simple, structured timeline—it turns surprises into leverage.

Property intelligence isn't just about avoiding mistakes—it's about getting better deals.

Once you've completed your checklist, you'll have something incredibly valuable: negotiation strength. Property intelligence isn't just about avoiding mistakes—it's about getting better deals. In the next chapter, you'll learn exactly how to use this information to negotiate effectively.

Chapter 12 Key Takeaways

□ A seven-category checklist ensures you evaluate every critical risk factor before making an offer

□ The Go/No-Go framework turns data into clear decisions aligned with your risk tolerance

□ A seven-day timeline keeps the process simple, organized, and efficient

□ Start with deal-breakers to avoid wasted time on properties that won't work

□ Batch tasks and stay organized to make research faster with each property

□ Hot markets require focus on the most relevant categories first, then complete the rest

□ Your findings directly influence negotiation strategy—knowledge creates leverage

----

Chapter Resources

Feel free to skip ahead if you'd like to continue reading.

Run the Checklist Before You Write the Offer.

You now have a complete pre-offer checklist. The next step? Actually use it.

At **HomeDataReports.com**, we've built this entire checklist into our comprehensive reports. Every Essential and Comprehensive Report includes flood analysis, hurricane risk, seismic hazards, wildfire scores, environmental proximity data, climate projections, and neighborhood trends—the exact checklist you just learned.

Create your free account and download your first Essential Report at no cost. Run our risk calculator on every property you're seriously considering—it takes 30 seconds and gives you an instant pass/fail on major risk categories. Download our Chrome extension so you can run this checklist in real-time while browsing listings online.

For real estate agents: Imagine handing your buyers a pre-offer checklist report for every property they're considering. Our partner program lets you do exactly that—it positions you as a thorough, data-driven advisor and prevents deals from falling apart due to surprises during inspections or insurance applications.

Share this chapter—and the checklist—with friends, family, and colleagues. Running this checklist before making an offer can save tens of thousands of dollars and months of stress.

This is the system. Now use it. Start at **HomeDataReports.com**

Chapter 13

Turning Data Into Negotiation Power

The first time you negotiate with real data in your hands, the conversation feels different.

A couple in San Francisco made an offer on a two-bedroom condo listed at $1,449,000. The unit was beautiful—light, views, prime location. But instead of leading with emotion, their agent led with evidence.

They pulled comprehensive property intelligence: FEMA flood maps, insurance quotes, traffic volume data, days-on-market history, and comparable sales. They documented that this property faced higher insurance costs, offered no dedicated parking, and had already taken a price reduction after sitting longer than comparable units.

Their initial offer: $1,325,000. The seller countered. They responded—not with "we just feel it's overpriced"—but with calm facts: "Here's what we're actually buying: higher ongoing insurance, no parking, and longer resale time. Based on comparable data and true cost of ownership, this is the price that makes sense for us."

After several respectful rounds, they closed at $1,337,500. Total reduction from list: $111,500. The seller moved on. The buyer got a fair price. Nobody felt attacked.

Data is not a weapon. It is a shared map of reality that helps both sides arrive at a fair price.

The difference wasn't charm or aggression. It was documented, defensible data.

You now have access to that same information for any property: federal databases, insurance quotes, climate projections, environmental records, and neighborhood trends. The question in this chapter is simple: how do you turn all of that into negotiation power without turning the negotiation into a battle?

Why Most Buyers Negotiate from Weakness

When you negotiate without data, the power tilts toward whoever is more confident, more experienced, or more emotionally detached.

Sellers know the home's story. Your agent juggles multiple clients. You have the highest stakes and least experience. That leads to two extremes: accepting the asking price from fear of "losing the house," or throwing out a low offer with no justification.

Property intelligence changes that. When you show up with FEMA maps, EPA reports, wildfire scores, insurance quotes, and repair costs, you shift from feelings to facts.

Instead of "I think this is too high," you say: "This property costs more to own than comparable homes because of its risk profile. I'm asking for a price that matches the actual 30-year cost."

□ **ACTION STEP 1:** Before making your offer, compile your complete property intelligence: flood zone status, insurance quotes, environmental data, and comparable sales.

Buyers who negotiate using inspection findings alone save an average of $14,000 off asking price. Add location-based risks, insurance projections, and mitigation costs, and the leverage grows—especially in properties with flood, contamination, or wildfire exposure.

Your goal is not the lowest price. Your goal is the right price based on true cost of ownership.

Three Strategies for Data-Driven Negotiation

Strategy 1: Request a Price Reduction Based on Long-Term Cost

This is the most direct approach. It works best when the property has clear, quantifiable risks that increase ownership costs.

Document the additional expenses over the life of ownership. If flood insurance adds $3,000 per year, that's $90,000 over a 30-year mortgage. If the property requires a $15,000 mitigation system, that's money out of pocket at closing.

Present these numbers as financial reality, not complaints. Show that the list price doesn't reflect true ownership cost when factoring in risk mitigation and higher insurance.

□ **ACTION STEP 2:** Calculate the 30-year total cost difference between this property and comparable homes without the same risk factors.

Example: "Insurance quotes show annual premiums of $4,200 compared to $1,800 for similar homes outside the flood zone. Over 30 years, that's $72,000 additional. We'd like to adjust our offer to reflect that long-term impact."

Strategy 2: Request Seller-Funded Mitigation

If the seller won't budge on price, ask them to cover mitigation costs instead. This works when the property needs specific improvements—drainage systems, foundation reinforcement, wildfire-resistant landscaping.

Sellers often find it easier to agree to specific repairs than to lower the sale price. It feels less like "losing money" and more like solving a problem.

□ **ACTION STEP 3:** Get written quotes for mitigation work before negotiation so you can request specific dollar amounts for seller credits.

Example: "We understand you'd prefer not to reduce the price. We've received a quote for $12,500 to install proper drainage. Would you provide a credit at closing to cover this mitigation work?"

Strategy 3: Build Contingencies Into Your Offer

When the seller refuses both price adjustments and mitigation credits, protect yourself through contingencies. These are conditions that must be met before the sale finalizes—giving you legal exit routes if problems escalate.

Common risk-based contingencies:

- **Insurance contingency:** Sale is contingent on securing homeowners insurance at or below a specified premium

- **Final inspection contingency:** Right to a final walkthrough; can withdraw if conditions have worsened

- **Appraisal contingency:** Sale depends on the home appraising at or above the agreed price

□ **RED FLAG #1:** If a seller refuses all three approaches—no price reduction, no mitigation credit, and no contingencies—they're not negotiating in good faith. Consider walking away.

□ **ACTION STEP 4:** Work with your agent to include specific contingencies in your purchase agreement based on the property's documented risks.

The three strategies give you flexibility: negotiate price first, request mitigation funding second, and protect yourself with contingencies third.

Using Your Data in Real Conversations

Script 1: Opening Negotiation with Risk Data

"We're very interested in the property. Based on federal flood maps, this home sits in a high-risk zone. Insurance quotes show premiums around $3,800 annually—significantly higher than comparable homes outside the flood zone. Over 30 years, that's more than $110,000 additional. We'd like to work on a price that reflects this long-term expense."

Script 2: Responding to Seller Pushback

"We appreciate your perspective. We're not questioning the home's value—the structure and location are exactly what we want. We're addressing documented risk that increases our costs. These aren't opinions—they're quotes from insurance companies and federal agencies. We're asking for a fair adjustment that accounts for the financial reality we'll face."

□ **ACTION STEP 5:** Practice your negotiation language with your agent before presenting it to ensure you sound confident and professional.

Script 3: Requesting Seller-Funded Repairs

"We've reviewed the environmental reports. The EPA Superfund site proximity requires professional assessment. We've obtained a quote for $8,500 for soil testing and remediation planning. Would you provide a closing credit to cover this work?"

Script 4: Walking Away Professionally

"After reviewing all available data and considering the risks, we cannot move forward at the current price without additional mitigation or contingencies. If circumstances change, we remain interested. Thank you."

Walking away is not failure. It's protecting yourself from a purchase that doesn't serve your long-term interests.

□ **ACTION STEP 6:** Set your walk-away price before negotiations begin and commit to it—don't let emotions override your financial boundaries.

Handling Seller Objections Like a Pro

Even with solid data, sellers push back. Here's how to respond without escalating tension.

Objection 1: "Other buyers didn't have a problem with this."

Response: "Every buyer evaluates risk differently based on their financial situation and insurance options. We've done our research and received actual quotes. We're committed to making a smart long-term decision."

Objection 2: "The price is already fair for the market."

Response: "We agree the home is priced fairly compared to similar listings. We're addressing that this property carries higher ongoing costs due to documented risks. We're comparing it to the total cost of ownership over 30 years."

□ **RED FLAG #2:** If the seller dismisses federal data or insurance quotes as "just opinions," they're not negotiating based on facts. This is a warning sign about their transparency.

Objection 3: "I've already dropped the price once."

Response: "We appreciate that adjustment. However, the risk factors we're addressing weren't reflected in that reduction. Flood zone designation, insurance costs, and environmental proximity are specific to this property. We're asking for an adjustment that addresses those documented concerns."

Objection 4: "You're being too picky."

Response: "We respect this is a significant decision for you. It's equally significant for us. We're not trying to be difficult—we're trying to make an informed decision based on real data. These aren't preferences; they're documented risks affecting long-term costs."

□ **ACTION STEP 7:** Keep all negotiations respectful and fact-based—never make it personal or attack the seller's decisions.

Professional data presentation isn't aggressive—it's smart business. Sellers respect buyers who've done their homework and lead with facts, not emotion.

When to Walk Away and When to Compromise

Walk away if:

- The seller refuses to acknowledge documented risks from federal agencies
- You cannot secure affordable insurance at any price point
- Mitigation costs exceed your budget and the seller won't help
- Hidden issues emerge during inspection
- Your gut tells you something isn't right

□ **RED FLAG #3:** Trust your instincts. If a seller is defensive, evasive, or hostile during negotiations, it's a preview of how they'll handle problems after closing.

Consider compromise if:

- The seller agrees to partial mitigation funding
- Insurance costs are manageable with proper coverage adjustments
- The property offers unique benefits that outweigh documented risks
- You can structure contingencies that protect your interests
- The seller negotiates in good faith even if they can't meet all requests

□ **ACTION STEP 8:** Create a written list of "must-haves" versus "nice-to-haves" before negotiation—this keeps you focused on what truly matters.

A good deal is one where both sides feel respected and neither side feels taken advantage of.

This book isn't about scaring you away from homes. It's about giving you the information to make decisions that are right for you. When you negotiate with data, you're not being difficult—you're being smart.

Real Outcome: Data-Driven Negotiation in Action

A buyer in San Francisco's Hayes Valley made an offer on a two-bedroom condo listed at $1,449,000. Instead of negotiating on emotion, they presented comprehensive data:

- Flood risk analysis showing higher insurance costs
- Comparable sales data from quieter streets with dedicated parking
- Days-on-market trends showing the property had been sitting longer than similar units
- Traffic volume documentation affecting long-term quality of life

Initial asking price: $1,449,000 **Buyer's initial offer:** $1,325,000 **Final negotiated price:** $1,337,500 **Total savings:** $111,500

The seller appreciated the professionalism and transparency. The buyer closed confidently, fully aware of the true long-term costs. This is the power of data presented respectfully—it creates clarity, lowers tension, and leads to fair agreements for everyone involved.

Professional data presentation isn't aggressive—it's smart business. Sellers respect buyers who've done their homework and lead with facts, not emotion.

Chapter 13 Key Takeaways

□ Data shifts negotiation from emotion to facts—use federal databases and insurance quotes as your foundation

□ Three strategies give you flexibility: price reduction, seller-funded mitigation, or protective contingencies

□ Professional scripts keep negotiations respectful while protecting your interests

□ Expect seller objections and respond calmly with documented evidence

□ Know your walk-away point before negotiations begin and stick to it

□ Data-driven negotiation can save tens of thousands while keeping the process respectful

□ A fair deal is one where both sides feel respected and neither feels taken advantage of

Negotiation is only one part of protecting yourself financially. Property intelligence doesn't end at closing—it continues throughout ownership. In the final chapter, we'll cover ongoing monitoring: how to track risks, stay ahead of insurance changes, and protect your investment for years to come.

Chapter Resources

Feel free to skip ahead if you'd like to continue reading.

Negotiate with Confidence—Backed by Federal Data.

You just learned how to turn property intelligence into negotiation leverage. Now it's time to put that into practice with real reports, real data, and real savings.

When you create your free account at **HomeDataReports.com**, you get access to the exact data sources used in successful negotiations: FEMA flood maps, insurance quotes, environmental proximity reports, seismic hazard data, and climate projections. Our comprehensive reports are designed to be shared with sellers, agents, and lenders—they're professional, defensible, and backed by federal data.

Download your first Essential Report free when you sign up. Use our risk calculator to identify negotiation points before you make an offer. Download our Chrome extension to evaluate properties and build your negotiation strategy in real-time.

For realtors and buyer's agents: Data-driven negotiation is your competitive advantage. Join our partner network and provide clients with comprehensive property intelligence reports that strengthen their offers and protect their interests. Many agents now include a PropertyRiskReport with every offer—it shows sellers you're serious, informed, and working with facts, not emotions.

Share this chapter with anyone preparing to make an offer. Negotiation backed by federal data isn't aggressive—it's smart business.

Want to see real negotiation examples using property intelligence reports? Our video masterclass includes case studies and scripts you can adapt for your own transactions. Check it out at **HomeDataReports.com**

Chapter 14

Beyond Closing Day — Annual Monitoring & Long-Term Strategy

Sarah almost missed the letter.

It came in the middle of a busy week—kids' activities, work deadlines, overflowing inbox. The envelope from the county floodplain office looked generic enough that she almost set it aside. But she had a habit she'd started the year they bought their home: every year, on their closing anniversary, she did a simple "property intelligence checkup."

So she opened it.

The letter explained that new FEMA maps were coming, and her street was part of a proposed expansion of the Special Flood Hazard Area. The maps weren't final yet, but if the change stood, her home would be officially "in the flood zone" the following year.

Most homeowners in her neighborhood did not find out until their mortgage company sent a notice: "Flood insurance now required. Please provide proof within 45 days or we will add lender-placed insurance to your loan." The quotes they received were around $3,500 per year—on top of their existing homeowners policy.

Sarah had a full year of runway.

She used that time to get an elevation certificate, talk with a flood expert, and confirm that her home actually sat higher than parts of the new mapped area. That evidence helped her file an appeal, and the final map line ended up across the street instead of through her living room. Even if the appeal had not worked, she and her husband already had a plan for flood insurance costs and mitigation.

Same neighborhood. Same maps. Same risk.

The difference was that Sarah treated property intelligence as ongoing maintenance, not a one-time pre-closing project—just like you learned to do with wildfire and insurance markets earlier in the book.

Property intelligence isn't a one-time event. Markets change, maps update, and risks evolve. Annual monitoring keeps you protected.

Why Monitoring Matters After You Close

By this point, you've done the heavy lifting. You learned how to research risk (Chapters 1-11), use a checklist before you make an offer (Chapter 12), and negotiate with data (Chapter 13).

It would be easy to think, "Great—that's done. On to paint colors and furniture."

But the data around your property does not freeze on closing day. Flood maps change as FEMA updates lines based on shifting rainfall patterns, sea levels, and drainage systems. Wildfire and hurricane models evolve annually as insurers adjust their calculations based on recent disasters and new science. Insurance markets move as carriers enter and exit counties, change underwriting standards, or introduce new deductibles long before a headline-making disaster happens. Property values respond when an area is newly mapped into a flood or high-fire zone—values can drop and appreciation can slow, even if nothing physical about the home has changed.

You do not need to watch maps and headlines every week. That would be exhausting and unnecessary.

What you do need is a calm, repeatable, two-hour routine once a year that keeps you a step ahead—so you never wake up to surprise costs, forced insurance, or risk designations you could have seen coming.

☐ **ACTION STEP 1:** Set a calendar reminder for your closing anniversary—this is your annual property intelligence review date.

Think of this like changing your air filters or scheduling an annual physical. You're not living in fear—you're just being a responsible owner.

Your Annual Monitoring Checklist

Once a year, block out two hours on a Saturday morning or Sunday afternoon and run through this process. It does not require special software or professional help. Just you, a laptop, and the same federal websites you used before you bought.

Check FEMA Flood Maps: Visit the FEMA Flood Map Service Center and enter your address. Look for any notices about pending or proposed map changes. If FEMA is updating your area's maps, you will typically see a preliminary version posted months before it becomes official. Early notice gives you time to respond.

□ **ACTION STEP 2:** Revisit FEMA's Flood Map Service Center annually to check for preliminary or updated maps in your area.

Review Your Insurance Coverage: Pull out your homeowners, flood, earthquake, and any other hazard policies. Check your premiums, deductibles, and coverage limits. Compare them to last year. If premiums jumped significantly or a carrier sent a non-renewal notice, that is a signal the market is shifting. Research shows that insurance companies often adjust rates and coverage availability based on evolving risk models, sometimes years before a major event occurs in an area.

□ **RED FLAG #1:** Premium increases over 15% year-over-year or non-renewal notices signal a hardening insurance market—time to shop alternatives or consider mitigation.

Monitor Wildfire and Hurricane Risk Updates: If you live in a wildfire or hurricane zone, check the latest risk maps. California's Fire Hazard Severity Zones are updated periodically, and hurricane wind maps evolve as climate patterns shift. These updates can affect both insurance and property values.

Track Local Infrastructure and Development: New developments, drainage projects, or infrastructure changes near your property can influence flood risk, traffic patterns, and neighborhood character. Local government websites often post updates on zoning changes, planned construction, and stormwater management projects.

□ **ACTION STEP 3:** Review your current insurance policies—compare premiums, deductibles, and coverage to last year's policies.

Review Property Value Trends: Use online tools to see how comparable homes in your area are selling. If properties with similar risk profiles are selling at discounts, that is a market signal. If values are holding steady or increasing despite known risks, that can indicate strong mitigation efforts or buyer confidence.

Annual monitoring is not about obsessing over data—it's about staying informed enough to make proactive decisions instead of reactive ones.

This entire process takes less time than a trip to the grocery store, and it can save you thousands of dollars or help you make strategic decisions with months or years of runway instead of weeks.

☐ **ACTION STEP 4:** Check wildfire or hurricane risk maps if applicable to your region—look for updates to hazard zones.

Long-Term Strategic Thinking

Ongoing monitoring is not just about avoiding surprises. It is also about positioning yourself to make smart long-term decisions—whether that means investing in mitigation, refinancing, renovating, or even selling at the right time.

Mitigation as Value Protection: When you spot early signs of insurance market tightening or new risk designations, you have time to invest in mitigation. Installing hurricane shutters, upgrading to impact-resistant windows, or creating defensible space around your home can reduce premiums and protect property value. Research indicates that homes with documented mitigation measures often command higher resale values and attract more buyer interest in high-risk areas.

A homeowner in a wildfire-prone Western community noticed neighbors losing coverage as insurers tightened underwriting. Instead of waiting, he invested in defensible space, a fire-resistant roof, and documented his mitigation efforts. When some carriers left the market, his improved risk profile helped him maintain coverage options and avoid the steepest premium increases that affected less-prepared neighbors.

Refinancing and Risk: If you are considering refinancing, understanding your current risk profile matters. Lenders may require updated elevation certificates, new appraisals, or additional insurance if risk maps have changed since you bought. Knowing this ahead of time helps you plan accordingly and avoid delays.

☐ **ACTION STEP 5:** If considering refinancing or major renovations, review any updated risk maps or insurance requirements first.

Selling with Transparency: If you decide to sell, you will be required to disclose known hazards in most states. Regular monitoring means you already have the documentation and can present risks transparently—along with any mitigation you have completed. Transparency builds trust with buyers and can actually strengthen your negotiating position.

Exit Strategy When Needed: Sometimes, ongoing monitoring reveals that a market is shifting in ways that do not align with your long-term goals. In coastal areas where new flood maps and rising premiums slowly reduce buyer demand, early information gives you options. You can choose to sell while your home still carries a modest adjustment instead of a deep discount, and reinvest in a lower-risk area that better aligns with your financial goals.

□ **RED FLAG #2:** Multiple comparable homes in your area selling at significant discounts due to risk factors—consider whether your long-term strategy still aligns with the property.

Strategic Renovation Decisions: If you are planning major renovations, monitoring helps you make smarter choices. Adding a second story in a flood zone? Elevation matters. Building an addition in a wildfire area? Material selection and defensible space become critical. Long-term data informs better decisions.

Strategic homeownership means making decisions based on evolving information, not reacting to crises.

□ **ACTION STEP 6:** Document any mitigation efforts you complete—this creates value for insurance discounts and future resale.

Real-World Strategic Moves

Here are a few ways real homeowners have used ongoing monitoring to make smart long-term decisions:

Appeal and Stay: A Massachusetts owner learned—months after closing—that updated FEMA maps moved her into a high-risk flood zone. Because she had already built the habit of checking official data, she quickly gathered elevation documents and worked with a specialist to appeal the designation. The result: she removed the mandatory insurance requirement and protected both her monthly budget and resale value.

Mitigate and Hold: In a wildfire-prone community in the West, a homeowner saw neighbors losing coverage as insurers tightened underwriting. Instead of waiting, he used this as a signal to invest in defensible space, a fire-resistant roof, and documented mitigation. When some carriers left the market, his improved risk profile helped him keep options and avoid the steepest premium increases.

Exit Strategically: In a coastal area where new flood maps and rising premiums were slowly reducing buyer demand, one family watched the pattern over several years. When they saw nearby sales starting to reflect significant flood-related discounts, they chose to sell while their home still carried a modest adjustment instead of a deep discount. They reinvested in a lower-risk inland neighborhood, protecting their equity.

In each case, the key advantages were the same: **early information, calm analysis, and deliberate action**. You may not be able to change the maps—but with ongoing property intelligence, you can decide how and when to respond in a way that protects your family and your long-term financial picture.

You may not be able to change the maps—but with ongoing monitoring, you can decide how and when to respond.

The Bigger Picture: You're Not Just a Homeowner Anymore

You've reached the end of this book, but you are not at the end of your journey. In many ways, this is the beginning of a new chapter in how you approach one of the biggest financial decisions of your life.

You now speak a language most buyers never learn. You understand how to read maps, analyze risk, project long-term costs, and make decisions rooted in clarity—not emotion or pressure. That alone places you in the top tier of informed homeowners and investors.

Most people buy homes hoping everything works out. You no longer need to hope. You can verify. You can analyze. You can choose with confidence. That is the essence of empowered homeownership.

The difference between an uninformed buyer and an informed one isn't intelligence—it's process.

The difference between an uninformed buyer and an informed one is not intelligence—it is process. Uninformed buyers depend on luck. Informed buyers depend on information. You have built that foundation, step by step, chapter by chapter.

And as we have said throughout this book, this was never about fear. This was never about avoiding properties with risk. It was about **understanding** them. A flood zone is not a dealbreaker if you know the insurance cost and factor it into your offer. A wildfire-prone area can be a wonderful place to live if you commit to proper mitigation. A seismic zone is manageable with the right retrofit and coverage. What matters most is alignment—your goals, your budget, your long-term plan, and the data that guides you toward the right decision for your family.

This book wasn't about scaring you away from homes. It was about giving you the tools to make decisions that are right for YOU.

One of the most powerful examples of this comes from a homeowner in Massachusetts who purchased a property that later appeared—unexpectedly—on a new FEMA preliminary map. Many neighbors discovered this only when their lenders notified them of a mandatory flood insurance requirement costing thousands annually. But this homeowner had been monitoring the maps. She caught the proposed change early, obtained an elevation certificate, filed an appeal, and ultimately had the final map line shifted off her property. Her proactive approach protected both her budget and her home value—saving tens of thousands of dollars over the coming years. Knowledge did not cause fear. It created options.

Your Next Steps

Your next steps are simple.

Start your next home search by checking risk maps before you ever schedule a showing. If you already own a home, complete your first annual property intelligence review this weekend. Share what you have learned with someone you care about—a friend, family member, or colleague who is thinking about buying. And when you need a deeper, comprehensive analysis, HomeDataReports.com is here to support you with clarity and accuracy.

□ **RED FLAG #3:** Discovering risk data for the first time AFTER closing—avoid this by making monitoring an annual habit starting now.

You have the tools. You have the knowledge. You have the framework. Now it is time to use them.

The most expensive homes are the ones you buy without knowing what you're actually buying. Now you know better—and you can choose better.

The most expensive homes are the ones you buy without knowing what you are actually buying. Now you know better—and you can choose better.

Welcome to informed, empowered homeownership. The journey continues from here.

Chapter 14 Key Takeaways

□ Property intelligence is ongoing—set an annual review date to monitor risk maps, insurance markets, and property values

□ Early warning gives you time to mitigate, appeal, or adjust your strategy instead of reacting to crises

□ Use monitoring to inform long-term decisions: renovation, refinancing, mitigation, or strategic exit

□ Document all mitigation efforts—they create value for insurance discounts and future resale

□ Strategic homeownership means making proactive decisions based on evolving information

□ You now have the tools and knowledge to make confident, informed decisions for life

□ Share what you've learned—help others avoid costly surprises and make smarter choices

----

Chapter Resources

Feel free to skip ahead if you'd like to continue reading.

Monitor Your Property's Risk—Every Year.

Closing day isn't the end of your property intelligence journey—it's the beginning. FEMA updates flood maps. Insurance markets shift. Climate projections evolve. Annual monitoring keeps you ahead of changes that could cost thousands.

At **HomeDataReports.com**, we make annual monitoring simple. Run a new report once a year (or whenever you're considering refinancing, renovating, or selling) to see updated flood maps, insurance market trends, climate projections, and environmental data.

Create your free account and download your first Essential Report at no cost. Set a calendar reminder for your closing anniversary and run a fresh report annually—it takes 10 minutes and can reveal changes that affect your property value, insurance costs, or long-term strategy. Download our Chrome extension to monitor nearby properties and market trends in real-time.

For financial advisors and mortgage lenders: Annual property monitoring is a valuable service you can offer clients during refinancing conversations or portfolio reviews. Join our partner network and provide updated property intelligence reports as part of your ongoing client relationships.

Share **HomeDataReports.com** with homeowners who closed years ago and haven't checked federal data since. Markets change, maps update, and risks evolve—annual monitoring protects long-term equity.

Our digital toolkit includes annual monitoring checklists and templates you can use to stay organized. Available at **HomeDataReports.com**

Chapter 15

Final Thoughts

You see it now, don't you?

You can't look at a listing the same way anymore. You can't scroll past a beautiful exterior photo without wondering what the flood maps say. You can't read "charming coastal cottage" without thinking about storm surge projections. You can't see "mountain views" without considering wildfire evacuation routes.

You've learned to see what other buyers miss.

And that changes everything.

The Journey You Just Took

Over the last several chapters, you've built something most homebuyers never develop: **a systematic framework for evaluating property risk using authoritative data sources.**

You learned **how to read FEMA flood maps**—not just whether a property is in a flood zone, but what that zone actually means, how Base Flood Elevation works, what insurance will cost, and when you should appeal a designation.

You learned **how hurricanes, storm surge, and coastal risks actually work**—the difference between wind damage and water damage, why elevation matters more than distance from shore, and how to interpret NOAA's Sea Level Rise projections for 30-year ownership timelines.

You learned **how to evaluate earthquake zones**—what seismic hazard maps actually show, why liquefaction risk matters more than fault line proximity, and how California's different building codes create vastly different risk profiles.

You learned **where wildfires are expanding and why**—how to read fire history maps, what the Wildland-Urban Interface means, why defensible space requirements exist, and when insurance companies withdraw from entire regions.

You learned **what environmental contamination data you need to check**—how far is too close to a Superfund site, what the EPA's National Priorities List means, why radon zones matter, and when off-site hazards affect property values.

You learned **how climate change projections affect long-term property decisions**—what 30-year precipitation changes mean for your basement, how temperature trends impact HVAC costs, and why some areas are becoming fundamentally uninsurable.

You learned **what your insurance company knows that you don't**—how carriers evaluate risk differently than appraisers, why some properties get denied coverage before you even make an offer, and what "non-renewal" means for your financial planning.

Most importantly, you learned **how to think like an informed buyer instead of a hopeful one.**

That's not a small shift. That's the difference between discovering six-figure problems after closing and understanding risks before you sign.

You're Not Ignorant Anymore

Here's what I hope changed while reading this book:

You're not trusting seller disclosures anymore. You know they only reveal what sellers are aware of—and sellers who deliberately avoid inspections can legally claim ignorance.

You're not assuming "the inspector will catch it" anymore. You know home inspectors don't check flood maps, don't pull EPA databases, don't analyze climate projections, and don't research insurance availability.

You're not relying on your agent to tell you about risks anymore. You know most agents don't understand federal data sources, don't know how to interpret seismic hazard maps, and can't predict insurance costs two years from now.

You're not making offers based on listing photos and gut feelings anymore. You know the most important information isn't in the MLS description—it's in federal databases that have been publicly available for years.

You know what to look for. And that changes which properties you seriously consider.

Some homes that looked perfect on Zillow now raise immediate red flags. Other properties that seemed risky at first glance turn out to have manageable, quantifiable risks you're comfortable accepting.

You're not guessing anymore. You're not hoping for the best. You're not trusting that "everything will probably be fine."

You're making informed decisions based on authoritative data. And that puts you ahead of 95% of homebuyers who are still buying based on hope and incomplete information.

What You Do With This Knowledge

The real question isn't whether you learned something. The real question is: **what are you going to do with it?**

Here's my recommendation:

Start researching properties differently.

Before you fall in love with a house, before you schedule a showing, before you even call your agent—pull the data.

Check the FEMA flood zone. Look up historical storm events. Review EPA environmental records within a three-mile radius. Verify wildfire risk if you're in fire-prone regions. Check USGS seismic hazard maps if you're in earthquake country.

Get insurance quotes **before** making offers. Not after. Not during escrow when you're emotionally committed. Before.

Run the numbers on long-term costs—not just the mortgage payment, but insurance premiums, potential flood coverage, climate adaptation expenses, and maintenance costs driven by environmental exposure.

Make informed decisions about which risks you're willing to accept.

Because here's the truth: **every home has risks.** A house in a quiet suburban neighborhood with no flood zone, no wildfire threat, and no seismic activity still has risks—foundation issues, roof problems, aging systems, market downturns.

The goal was never to find a risk-free property. **The goal was to understand the specific risks of properties you're considering—and decide which ones align with your budget, your risk tolerance, and your long-term plans.**

A flood zone might be a dealbreaker for one family but perfectly acceptable to another who's budgeted for insurance and wants that specific location.

A wildfire-prone area might be off-limits for some buyers but an ideal choice for others who are committed to proper mitigation and love the mountain lifestyle.

This book gave you the tools to make those decisions with complete awareness instead of blind hope.

The Resources You'll Need

You've learned the frameworks. Now you need the data.

For comprehensive property intelligence: Visit **HomeDataReports.com** to generate detailed risk assessment reports that do the heavy lifting for you. Our platform aggregates data from FEMA, NOAA, USGS, EPA, Census, and other federal sources into clear, readable reports for any address in the United States.

You **could** spend hours navigating federal databases, cross-referencing multiple sources, and trying to interpret technical data yourself. Or you could get a comprehensive report in minutes and use that time to evaluate what the risks actually mean for your specific situation.

We're working toward helping tens of thousands of property buyers every month across the country through HomeDataReports.com and our affiliated websites. The platform exists because buyers deserve access to the same data professionals use—without needing a geology degree to understand it.

For the complete system: If you want to learn how to **use** this property risk knowledge during negotiations, **Book 2** teaches you the execution side. How to structure inspection contingencies, how to convert findings into documented leverage, when to negotiate price reductions versus repair credits, and how to protect your earnest money if things go sideways.

Book 1 gives you the data foundation. Book 2 teaches you how to negotiate based on that data. Together, they create the complete strategic framework.

For what's coming next: We're building additional resources—advanced courses, video walkthroughs of real property analysis examples, tools and calculators that streamline the research process, templates for organizing your findings.

The goal isn't just to help you buy **one** house successfully. The goal is to give you frameworks that work for every real estate decision you'll make over the next 30 years—purchases, refinances, evaluating neighborhoods for family members, understanding market shifts, building investment portfolios.

This knowledge compounds. The more properties you analyze, the faster you get at spotting risks. The more markets you understand, the better your long-term decisions become.

One Last Thing

Most homebuyers will never read this book.

They'll make offers based on curb appeal and staged photos. They'll trust that sellers disclosed everything important. They'll assume their agent or inspector will catch any major issues. They'll discover flood insurance costs $6,000 annually three weeks before closing. They'll find out their property is in a wildfire evacuation zone during the first emergency alert.

They'll close on properties with risks they never saw coming—and spend years dealing with the financial and emotional consequences.

You're not going to be one of those buyers.

You know where to look now. You understand what the data means. You've seen the patterns. You know which risks are manageable with proper planning and which ones are dealbreakers regardless of how beautiful the kitchen looks.

All that's left is execution.

So go find properties. Pull the data. Run the numbers. Evaluate the risks. Get insurance quotes. Compare long-term costs. Make informed decisions about which properties align with your budget, your lifestyle, and your tolerance for specific risk types.

And when you find the right one—a property where you **understand and accept** the risks with full awareness—make your offer with confidence.

Not blind optimism. Not hopeful ignorance. **Confidence built on complete information.**

That's the difference this book makes. That's what knowledge creates when applied systematically.

You've got the tools. You understand the data sources. You're ready.

Now go see what other buyers miss.

— **Damian Martinez**
Founder, HomeDataReports.com

Continue your education:

HomeDataReports.com: Comprehensive property intelligence reports for any U.S. address

Book 2: Strategic negotiation and transaction execution

Future releases: Advanced analysis courses, tools, and resources for informed buyers

You don't buy homes the same way anymore. You buy them better.

Chapter Resources

Feel free to skip ahead if you'd like to continue reading.

You're Ready. Now Take Action.

You've reached the end of the book, but you're just at the beginning of informed, empowered homeownership.

Everything you've learned—flood analysis, hurricane risk, seismic hazards, wildfire scores, environmental data, climate projections, demographic trends, negotiation strategies, and annual monitoring—is available right now at **HomeDataReports.com**

We built these platforms because we believe every homebuyer deserves access to the same federal data that professionals use—without needing a PhD in geology, climatology, or environmental science to interpret it. Think of it as a comprehensive intelligence report for homes—pulling data from 10+ federal sources into a single, actionable analysis you can use to make better decisions.

Here's what happens when you create your free account:

□ Get your first Essential Report completely free

□ Test our proprietary risk calculator on unlimited properties

□ Download our free Chrome extension for instant property intelligence while browsing listings

□ Access tools designed for negotiation, due diligence, and annual monitoring

□ Join a community of informed buyers who refuse to make six-figure decisions in the dark

For professionals—realtors, lenders, insurance agents, home inspectors, contractors:

Our partner referral program is built for you. Offer comprehensive property intelligence reports to your clients as part of your service, earn referral income, and differentiate yourself in a crowded market. Clients trust advisors who provide data, not just opinions. Join the network at **HomeDataReports.com**

Go deeper with advanced training:

Audiobook version of this book for learning on the go

Video masterclass with step-by-step property analysis and negotiation strategies

Digital toolkit with templates, checklists, and advanced research guides

All available at **HomeDataReports.com**

Share this book and these tools with people you care about. Send the link to friends shopping for homes. Recommend it to family members considering a move. Tell your realtor, lender, and insurance agent about the platform—many are already using it to serve their clients better.

Property intelligence isn't a luxury. It's a necessity. You now have the knowledge. You now have the tools. The only question left is: will you use them?

Start today at **HomeDataReports.com**

Your future self—and your bank account—will thank you.

Chapter 16

Appendix: Essential Resources & References

This book draws on federal databases, legal cases, insurance industry data, and real-world examples. Below are the key resources you need to conduct your own property intelligence research.

Federal Data Sources

These free government resources provide the foundation for property risk analysis:

FEMA (Federal Emergency Management Agency) Flood maps, disaster history, flood insurance data https://msc.fema.gov (Flood Map Service Center) https://www.floodsmart.gov (National Flood Insurance Program)

NOAA (National Oceanic and Atmospheric Administration) Climate data, sea-level rise projections, hurricane zones https://coast.noaa.gov/slr (Sea Level Rise Viewer) https://www.noaa.gov

USGS (United States Geological Survey) Earthquake zones, sinkholes, landslides, geological hazards https://earthquake.usgs.gov (Earthquake Hazards Program) https://www.usgs.gov

EPA (Environmental Protection Agency) Superfund sites, toxic releases, contamination data https://www.epa.gov/emefdata/em4ef.home (EnviroMapper) https://www.epa.gov

U.S. Census Bureau Demographics, economic trends, neighborhood data https://www.census.gov

State & Local Resources

State Insurance Departments Market bulletins, consumer resources, rate information

Search: "[Your State] Department of Insurance"

State Geological Surveys Local hazard data, soil maps, specialized reports Search: "[Your State] Geological Survey"

Local Building Departments Permit records, code enforcement, inspection history Visit your county/city government website

Floodplain Administrators Local flood mapping, elevation certificates, appeals Contact through your county or city government

Home Inspection Standards

ASHI (American Society of Home Inspectors) Professional standards defining inspection scope https://www.homeinspector.org/Standards-of-Practice

InterNACHI (International Association of Certified Home Inspectors) Alternative inspection standards and guidelines https://www.nachi.org/standards-of-practice

> Home inspections follow standardized protocols that exclude many location-based risks. This book teaches you to fill those gaps using federal data.

Real Estate Disclosure Laws

Disclosure requirements vary significantly by state. Most states require sellers to disclose only what they personally know—not what federal databases reveal.

State-Specific Requirements:

- California: Natural Hazard Disclosure Statement required
- Florida: Sinkhole and flood zone disclosure required
- Texas: Minimal mandatory disclosure
- Other states: Varies (research your state's requirements)

Resource: https://www.docjacket.com/resources/state-real-estate-disclosure-requirements

Insurance Resources

FloodSmart.gov National Flood Insurance Program information and quotes

Your State's FAIR Plan Last-resort insurance for high-risk properties Search: "[Your

State] FAIR Plan"

Insurance Information Institute Consumer guides and market information https://www.iii.org

CLUE Reports (Comprehensive Loss Underwriting Exchange) Property loss history (request through your insurance agent)

Legal Context

The case examples in this book represent real patterns in property disputes:

- **Construction defects:** Buyers often discover issues after closing that were documentable before purchase
- **Undisclosed hazards:** Sellers may not know about federal data showing flood, sinkhole, or contamination risks
- **Natural disasters:** Properties labeled "no flood risk" have experienced catastrophic flooding (Hurricane Helene, North Carolina, 2024)
- **Insurance denials:** Coverage gaps emerge when policies exclude specific perils (California wildfire smoke damage cases, 2024)

□ **LEGAL NOTE:** This book provides educational information, not legal advice. Consult an attorney for questions about contracts, disclosure requirements, or property disputes.

Case Study Notes

The personal stories throughout this book are composite examples representing common patterns documented in:

- Court records and legal filings
- Insurance industry data
- Real estate transaction data
- News reports and consumer complaints

Names, locations, and specific details are modified to protect privacy while illustrating real risks and outcomes.

Key Examples:

- Sarah and Daniel (Sinkhole): Represents typical Florida sinkhole disclosure gaps and $155,000 average repair costs
- Sarah and Mike (Negotiation): Demonstrates data-driven negotiation in Tampa market with typical flood insurance costs ($450/month)
- Massachusetts homeowner (FEMA appeal): Real pattern of successful map appeals using elevation certificates

Additional Support

HomeDataReports.com Comprehensive property intelligence reports aggregating 10+ federal data sources for any U.S. address

Ready.gov Federal emergency preparedness resources and guidance

Your Local Emergency Management Office Community-specific hazard information and evacuation plans

Methodology Notes

Data Accuracy: All federal data sources cited are publicly accessible and updated regularly by government agencies. Information is current as of the book's publication date.

Statistics: Where statistics are cited (e.g., "80% of homebuyers consider climate risk"), they represent synthesis of multiple industry surveys conducted 2023-2024.

Cost Estimates: Insurance premiums, mitigation costs, and property values reflect typical ranges documented in market data but vary significantly by location, property characteristics, and individual circumstances.

Using This Appendix

This appendix provides starting points for your own research. The federal websites listed here are free, authoritative, and updated regularly. Combined with local resources and professional guidance when needed, these tools give you the foundation for informed property decisions.

Quick Reference Checklist:

- ☐ Check FEMA flood maps before making an offer
- ☐ Review EPA Superfund sites within 1-3 miles
- ☐ Research earthquake/sinkhole/wildfire risk for your region
- ☐ Get insurance quotes early in your search process
- ☐ Review state disclosure laws to understand what sellers must reveal
- ☐ Set annual monitoring reminders for ongoing risk assessment

The difference between informed and uninformed homebuyers isn't access to data—it's knowing which data matters and how to use it.

About the Development of This Book

Modern Book Development Process

This book was created using AI-assisted writing tools to accelerate the drafting process and improve the organization and clarity of complex concepts. The workflow combined human expertise with AI capabilities:

Author Role:

Designed all chapter structures, analytical frameworks, and strategic methodologies

Provided source data, concepts, and direction for each section

Selected, modified, and approved all AI-generated content

Conducted fact-checking against federal databases and market research

Made final editorial decisions on all material included in the book

AI Tool Role:

Assisted with drafting text based on author-provided concepts and structures

Improved explanation clarity for technical topics

Enhanced organizational flow and readability

Accelerated conversion of ideas into structured written content

What AI Did NOT Do:

Originate the core risk analysis frameworks or negotiation strategies

Provide professional opinions or advice about specific properties

Make recommendations about transactions, contracts, or real estate decisions

Replace human judgment, expertise, or fact-checking

The resulting content reflects the author's perspectives, experience, and interpretation of publicly available federal data and real estate market dynamics. AI tools served as drafting assistants, not content creators or professional advisors.

Continued Disclaimer

As stated in the legal disclaimer at the beginning of this book, this material is provided solely for educational and informational purposes. It does not constitute legal, real estate, insurance, tax, engineering, or financial advice. Readers must consult licensed professionals before making any property-related decisions and remain fully responsible for their own choices and outcomes.

END OF APPENDIX

Chapter Resources

Feel free to skip ahead if you'd like to continue reading.

Chapter 17

Glossary of Terms

This glossary defines technical terms and acronyms used throughout the book to help you understand property risk data and federal databases.

A

AE Zone (Flood Zone AE)

A Special Flood Hazard Area with a 1% annual chance of flooding. Flood insurance is required for mortgaged properties in this zone. Base Flood Elevation (BFE) data is available.

All-Risk Policy (Insurance)

Insurance coverage that protects against all perils except those specifically excluded in the policy. Also called "open peril" coverage.

AO Zone (Flood Zone AO)

A Special Flood Hazard Area with sheet flow flooding (shallow flooding). Flood depths typically range from 1 to 3 feet.

Appraisal

A professional assessment of a property's market value, typically required by mortgage lenders before approving a loan.

B

Base Flood

A flood having a 1% chance of being equaled or exceeded in any given year (also known as the "100-year flood"). This is the flood standard used by FEMA for flood insurance requirements.

Base Flood Elevation (BFE)

The computed elevation to which floodwater is anticipated to rise during the base flood. Properties below this elevation face higher flood risk and insurance costs.

Brownfield

A property where redevelopment or reuse may be complicated by the presence or potential presence of hazardous substances, pollutants, or contaminants.

C

CLUE Report (Comprehensive Loss Underwriting Exchange)

A claims history database that tracks insurance claims filed on a property over the past 7 years. Used by insurance companies to assess risk.

Contingency

A condition that must be met before a real estate contract becomes binding. Common contingencies include financing, inspection, and appraisal.

Coverage Limit

The maximum amount an insurance policy will pay for a covered loss.

D

Deductible

The amount a policyholder must pay out-of-pocket before insurance coverage begins. Higher deductibles typically result in lower premiums.

Defensible Space

The area around a home where vegetation, debris, and other combustible materials are managed to reduce wildfire risk. Typically divided into zones extending 30-100 feet from structures.

Disclosure

Legal requirement for sellers to inform buyers of known material defects or hazards affecting a property. Requirements vary significantly by state.

E

Elevation Certificate

A survey document showing a property's elevation relative to Base Flood Elevation. Required for flood insurance in certain zones and used for LOMA applications.

EPA (Environmental Protection Agency)

Federal agency responsible for environmental protection, including oversight of Superfund sites, air and water quality, and hazardous waste management.

Escrow

A neutral third party that holds funds and documents during a real estate transaction until all conditions are met.

F

FAIR Plan (Fair Access to Insurance Requirements)

State-mandated insurance programs providing last-resort coverage for properties unable to obtain insurance in the standard market, typically due to high risk.

Fault Line

A fracture in Earth's crust along which movement has occurred. Active fault lines pose earthquake risk to nearby properties.

FEMA (Federal Emergency Management Agency)

Federal agency responsible for disaster response, flood insurance programs, and flood hazard mapping.

Fire Hazard Severity Zone (FHSZ)

California's classification system for wildfire risk, ranging from Moderate to Very High. Used for building codes, insurance underwriting, and disclosure requirements.

Flood Insurance Rate Map (FIRM)

Official FEMA map showing flood zones, Base Flood Elevations, and flood risk areas for a community.

Flood Zone

Geographic area classified by FEMA according to varying levels of flood risk. Zones A and V are high-risk; Zone X is moderate-to-low risk.

H

Hazard Mitigation

Actions taken to reduce or eliminate long-term risk from natural hazards. Examples include elevating structures, installing hurricane shutters, or creating defensible space.

L

Liquefaction

Soil behavior during earthquakes where saturated soil temporarily loses strength and behaves like a liquid, potentially causing buildings to sink or tilt.

LOMA (Letter of Map Amendment)

Official FEMA document removing a property from a Special Flood Hazard Area based on elevation data, eliminating mandatory flood insurance requirements.

M

Magnitude (Earthquake)

Measurement of earthquake size using the Richter scale or Moment Magnitude scale. Magnitude 5.0+ can cause damage; 7.0+ is considered major.

Modified Mercalli Intensity Scale

Scale measuring earthquake effects and damage, ranging from I (not felt) to XII (total destruction). Complements magnitude measurements.

N

Named Peril Policy

Insurance coverage that only protects against specific perils explicitly listed in the policy (e.g., fire, wind, hail). Less comprehensive than all-risk policies.

NFIP (National Flood Insurance Program)

Federal program administered by FEMA providing flood insurance to property owners, renters, and businesses in participating communities.

NOAA (National Oceanic and Atmospheric Administration)

Federal agency responsible for weather forecasting, climate monitoring, hurricane tracking, and sea-level rise projections.

NPL (National Priorities List)

EPA's list of most serious hazardous waste sites (Superfund sites) requiring long-term cleanup. Proximity to NPL sites can affect property values.

P

Peak Ground Acceleration (PGA)

Measure of earthquake ground shaking intensity. Higher PGA values indicate stronger shaking and greater potential damage.

Premium (Insurance)

The amount paid (usually annually or monthly) to maintain an insurance policy.

Preliminary Flood Map

Proposed FEMA flood map released for public review before becoming official, typically 12-18 months before finalization. Gives property owners time to appeal.

R

RCP (Representative Concentration Pathway)

Climate change scenarios used by scientists to project future greenhouse gas concentrations and their effects on temperature, sea level, and extreme weather.

RCRA (Resource Conservation and Recovery Act)

Federal law governing hazardous waste management. RCRA facilities store, treat, or dispose of hazardous materials and are tracked by EPA.

Resilience

A property's or community's ability to withstand and recover from natural disasters, climate impacts, or other stresses.

S

Saffir-Simpson Hurricane Wind Scale

Classification system rating hurricanes from Category 1 (74-95 mph winds) to Category 5 (157+ mph winds) based on sustained wind speed.

Sea-Level Rise

Increase in global ocean levels due to climate change, affecting coastal flooding, storm surge, and long-term property values.

Seismic Hazard

Earthquake-related risks including ground shaking, liquefaction, landslides, and surface rupture.

SFHA (Special Flood Hazard Area)

Areas with a 1% or greater annual chance of flooding (Flood Zones A and V). Flood insurance is required for mortgaged properties in these zones.

Storm Surge

Abnormal rise in water level during hurricanes or tropical storms caused by wind pushing water toward shore. Can cause severe coastal flooding.

Superfund Site

Contaminated location requiring long-term environmental cleanup, designated by EPA under CERCLA (Comprehensive Environmental Response, Compensation, and Liability Act).

T

TRI (Toxic Release Inventory)

EPA database tracking toxic chemical releases from industrial facilities. Publicly accessible and used to assess environmental risks near properties.

U

Underground Storage Tank (UST)

Tank and associated piping with at least 10% volume underground, typically used for petroleum or chemicals. Leaking USTs can contaminate soil and groundwater.

USGS (United States Geological Survey)

Federal scientific agency providing data on earthquakes, sinkholes, landslides, volcanoes, and geological hazards.

V

V Zone (Flood Zone V/VE)

Coastal high-hazard flood area subject to wave action and storm surge. Highest flood insurance rates and strictest building requirements. Flood insurance is mandatory for mortgaged properties.

VE Zone (Flood Zone VE)

V Zone with established Base Flood Elevation data, indicating high-velocity coastal flooding with wave action.

W

Wildland-Urban Interface (WUI)

Area where homes and wildland vegetation meet or intermix, creating elevated wildfire risk. Sometimes called the "ember zone."

X

X Zone (Flood Zone X)

Moderate-to-low flood risk area outside the Special Flood Hazard Area. Flood insurance is not required but is recommended and often affordable.

Shaded X Zone

Area of moderate flood risk (0.2% annual chance, or "500-year flood zone"). Historically about 25% of flood claims occur in X zones.

Unshaded X Zone

Area of minimal flood risk (less than 0.2% annual chance). Flood insurance is optional but may be wise in areas with changing flood patterns.

For more information on any of these terms, consult the referenced federal agencies:

FEMA: fema.gov

NOAA: noaa.gov

USGS: usgs.gov

EPA: epa.gov

END OF GLOSSARY

Chapter 18

About the Author

Damian Martinez is the founder of HomeDataReports.com, a platform dedicated to helping homebuyers make informed, data-driven decisions using comprehensive property intelligence reports.

After working as a licensed real estate agent from 2017 to 2019, Damian witnessed first-hand the critical gaps in the homebuying process—buyers making six-figure decisions with incomplete information, discovering costly surprises after closing, and relying on outdated disclosure systems that failed to protect their interests.

Frustrated by an industry that prioritized transactions over transparency, Damian left traditional real estate to build something better: a system that aggregates federal data from FEMA, NOAA, USGS, EPA, the U.S. Census Bureau, and other authoritative sources into actionable property intelligence reports accessible to every buyer, not just industry insiders.

In 2020, Damian purchased his own home using the exact methodology outlined in this book—checking flood maps, evaluating seismic risks, reviewing environmental data, and calculating long-term cost-of-ownership scenarios before making an offer. That experience validated what he already knew: informed buyers make better decisions.

Since founding HomeDataReports.com, Damian has helped tens of thousands of property buyers across the United States understand the risks associated with their potential purchases—not to discourage homeownership, but to empower buyers with the information they need to negotiate better, avoid preventable surprises, and choose properties that align with their goals and risk tolerance.

Damian's work is driven by a simple philosophy: every home has risks, but every buyer deserves to understand those risks before signing a contract. Property intelligence shouldn't be a luxury reserved for sophisticated investors or industry professionals—it should be accessible, understandable, and actionable for everyone.

When he's not analyzing property data or building new tools for homebuyers, Damian can be found in South Florida, refining the systems and strategies that help buyers across the country make smarter real estate decisions.

Learn more and access property intelligence tools at: HomeDataReports.com

Chapter 19

Your Next Step: Turn Knowledge Into Action

You've finished the book. Now it's time to put what you've learned to work.

Visit **HomeDataReports.com** and create your free account today. Here's what you get immediate access to:

Your First Essential Report - FREE

Generate a comprehensive property intelligence report for any U.S. address at no cost. See exactly what federal data reveals about flood zones, wildfire risk, earthquake hazards, environmental concerns, and climate projections.

Proprietary Risk Calculator

Test our advanced risk assessment tool on unlimited properties. Get instant risk scores across multiple categories before making offers or scheduling showings.

Free Chrome Extension

Install our browser extension and research properties in real-time while browsing Zillow, Realtor.com, or Redfin. One click pulls comprehensive risk data without leaving the listing page.

Partner Referral Network

Are you a realtor, lender, insurance agent, home inspector, or contractor? Join our partner network and provide professional-grade property intelligence to your clients. Build stronger relationships through better information.

Additional Resources

Digital Toolkit: Templates, calculators, checklists, and documentation guides

Video Masterclass: Real transaction examples with step-by-step walkthroughs

Audiobook Edition: Reinforce frameworks while commuting or researching properties

Future Releases: Advanced courses, investment strategies, and specialized market analysis

Share With Your Network

Know someone buying a home? Share HomeDataReports.com with friends, family, and colleagues. Help them make informed decisions backed by comprehensive data.

The Bottom Line

This book gave you the frameworks. The platform gives you the data.

Knowledge without execution is just theory. Data without strategy is just numbers.

You now have both.

Visit **HomeDataReports.com** today.

Create your account. Run your first report. Download the Chrome extension.

Start making real estate decisions the way informed buyers do—with complete awareness, strategic confidence, and authoritative data.

The American Dream deserves a foundation built on truth, not surprises.

HomeDataReports.com

Comprehensive property intelligence for every U.S. address.

Ready to Put This Knowledge to Work?

Ready to Put This Knowledge to Work? Scan to access:

- Your FREE property risk report
- The audiobook edition
- The digital toolkit
- The video masterclass
- And more resources for confident homebuyers at homedatareports.com/books

Made in the USA
Monee, IL
04 November 2026

67381910R00095